PLAYBOY PRESS EXECUTIVE LIBRARY

PSYCHO-CYBERNETICS AND THE STOCK MARKET

THE KEY TO MAXIMUM INVESTMENT PROFITS & PEACE OF MIND

CLAUDE N. ROSENBERG, JR.

Books by Claude N. Rosenberg, Jr.

Stock Market Primer

The Common Sense Way to Stock Market Profits

PSYCHO-CYBERNETICS AND THE STOCK MARKET

PSYCHO-CYBERNETICS AND THE STOCK MARKET

Published simultaneously in the United States and Canada by Playboy Press, Chicago, Illinois. Printed in the United States of America.

PLAYBOY and Rabbit Head design are trademarks of Playboy, 919 North Michigan Avenue, Chicago, Illinois 60611 (U.S.A.), Reg. U.S. Pat. Off., marca registrada, marque déposée.

Playboy Press hardcover edition published 1971. Playboy Press softcover edition published 1972.

Text design by Bob Antler.

To Weezy

ACKNOWLEDGMENTS

One of the great precepts in life is to avoid so-called tunnel vision, wherein you see things only from your own limited point of view.

Were it not for five people, I fear this work would have suffered from this very type of vision. When I commenced writing this book, I was convinced that the psychological elements of investing were the causes for the multitudes of failures experienced in stock investing, and that a process such as Psycho-Cybernetics could overcome these emotional hangups.

While the thesis was, and still is, correct, my use of Psycho-Cybernetics as it is normally understood was not correct. Fortunately I sought the counsel of others, who recognized that positive attitude was only a small part of the proper thinking process needed to overcome these psychological maladjustments concerning investments.

The first to tip me off was one of the great pros

of them all, Mr. Gerald M. Loeb, whose own book, *The Battle for Investment Survival,* is a classic and whose insights concerning our common interest will never be forgotten.

The second and third experts led me to understand that the mental feedback approach of Psycho-Cybernetics was the important thing and that a "Come up smiling" attitude, useful though it is in daily living, was secondary in accomplishing a specific task such as investing money wisely. Dr. Theodore Myers of San Francisco set these thoughts in motion—and then Dr. James A. Hamilton (also of San Francisco) really set me straight. Dr. Hamilton, a very practical psychiatrist, provided a critique which prompted me to rewrite what I had thought was finished work. All I can say is: thank goodness for all these inputs.

My fourth aid came from Mr. Leo Model, senior executive of the investment firm of Model, Roland & Co. of New York. Mr. Model has had many years of unusual success in the stock market and he understands investor psychology as well as anyone I know. Fortunately for me he was willing to share some of this knowledge, and his critique of my manuscript in its late stages was invaluable.

My final aid is really my first, my wife Louise, who understood the important criticisms of the abovementioned four and who kept me on the track from that time on.

If what follows has the practical value I am now confident it has, then these five people deserve real credit. Certainly they have my greatest appreciation.

CONTENTS

1. From Writer To Reader

Question: Do you *consistently* do the *right* things at the *right* time in the stock market?

If your answer to this is "Yes, practically all the time!" then this book is *not* for you.

If, however, you are in that vast majority—probably upwards of 95 percent—who have not truly maximized their investment dollars, then the next 208 pages should be the most important of your investment life.

Note what I said—that over 95 percent of the investing public fails to succeed handsomely in purchasing and selling stocks, which is indeed unfortunate. All of which leads to the logical query of why so many miss the proverbial boat. Stated more simply: why do *so many* do the *wrong* thing at the *wrong* time when it comes to stock investing?

Needless to say, an answer to this is hardly simple. There are obviously a vast number of ways to go wrong, and all are potentially responsible.

One crucial fact, however, is apparent—that this zigging when you should be zagging (and vice versa) *is strictly spontaneous.* My fifteen years in the business of making money in the stock market has shown me quite clearly that failure of others is quite automatic and is due to the mere fact of being *human.* Yes, the trouble with people in the stock market is that *they are people.*

Anyone doubting this need only look to 1970 and to the countless billions of dollars which were erased from portfolio assets. While some of this difficulty was due to economic, political, and social developments in the United States, close study shows that much was due to investor naïveté and stupidity. Even with all the real problems that existed, the market's break was largely due to human frailty.

This is not to say that, to succeed in the stock market, you are going to have to turn yourself into a giraffe or a coconut tree. But *you are going to have to rid yourself of certain human emotional reactions which tend to make you do the wrong thing at the wrong moment.*

In addition, you will want to accomplish an equally important goal: *to be relaxed and happy with your investments* rather than tense and nervous, which most people are. Thus, successful investing goes beyond dollar attainment. It is self-defeating to make a bundle of money if you become a bundle of nerves in the process.

Ridding ourselves of emotional reactions really sounds both too simple and too complex—at the same time—to be practical. It sounds too simple in that it is general, like saying that you have to be more efficient to succeed in life. And it sounds too complex in that altering human emotions is most difficult to perform. (After all, we can hardly count on changing everyone's personality.)

Fortunately, restructuring personality is not necessary—at least to accomplish the goals in mind. You can remain the same pleasant, well-adjusted dream of an individual you are—there is no need for basic change.

What then? What must we do to convert a normal, restrictive, and defeating reaction to stock investing into something that is positive, constructive, and enriching? Most important, what can we do *easily* to bring about this profitable conversion?

The answer lies in the chapters which follow. As you will see, the process is simple, involving a combination of:

1. A lot of good sense and logical thinking that have been passed down by people who have succeeded famously in the stock market over the years;
2. Conscious effort to understand and apply these thoughts and to convert the reader into the kind of intuitive investor who emerges from long years of successful experience; and, most important,
3. To provide the reader with a unique *thinking*

process which a large number of very successful people *in all walks of life* have utilized to their great advantage *in all types of applications. And then to relate this practical approach to the subject at hand —that of achieving both financial and emotional serenity.*

As you might expect, this is *not* a get-rich-quick book. As a matter of fact, all of the "How to Get Rich" books and all of the research recommendations emanating from brokers and investment services are really useless without the right psychological reactions. Thus, the crucial task is to convert to constructive and profitable ends the destructive emotions which have consistently inhibited investors. Which is just what *Psycho-Cybernetics and the Stock Market* should accomplish for you.

Furthermore, a correct understanding of your own investment makeup will provide you with a psychological insight into the actions of others—most particularly the other "players" in the stock-market "game." Needless to say, this understanding will afford you a strong competitive advantage.

Enough of the introduction. Let's get on to the method of thinking which is going to be the basis for a tremendous amount of general happiness in your daily life, too.

So let me share with you a way of thinking which has worked for me in both my everyday living and in making money—and which has been utilized by many dramatically successful people in all walks of life. . . .

2. Psycho-Cybernetics

Many of you already know of Psycho-Cybernetics, although I doubt that you have considered its use in the stock market. Many more of you have little or no knowledge of it at all.

If you are in the latter group, do not let the phrase frighten you. Understand right now that Psycho-Cybernetics is no deep philosophical or religious belief nor is it any form of hocus-pocus or anything complex.

Cybernetics (the forerunner of Psycho-Cybernetics) concerns itself with the control of human functions and with systems which can be designed to replace humans—like computers. Cybernetics assumes that any action directed towards a goal has to be controlled in order to achieve that goal; and that progress towards reaching the goal cannot be known without some form of communication. Like a helmsman who continuously adjusts the tiller of his boat to keep it on course, human actions of all sorts are controlled by constant feedback to the brain—which then reacts and adjusts for the data presented. All systems, therefore, utilize feedback. And if this feedback can be programmed correctly, there is no end to what might be accomplished.

Psycho-Cybernetics involves a logical extension of this thought. The term was originated by Dr. Maxwell Maltz of New York City, and it recognizes that man has a machine—his brain—which can be put to use to steer his behavior in all sorts of endeavors. By applying a number of proven scientific techniques, Psycho-Cybernetics capitalizes on the brain and the nervous system to accomplish some wonderful goals. Through this, an individual can improve his personality, his habits, his attitudes—and yet, as you will see, it is as simple and logical and practical as anything you have ever encountered.

For those of you who turn your noses up at the thought of "head shrinkers," I should inform you that the aforementioned Dr. Maltz is *not* a psychiatrist. He is a renowned plastic surgeon, who had observed how his scalpel served as a magic wand to alter both the physical appearance and the mental attitude of many individuals he had treated. He noted, however, how such surgery failed in many other cases to convince the person involved that appearance had been changed at all; and that many, many faces went on wearing the same old personalities as before.

What Dr. Maltz had recognized was the importance of *self-image*—the realization that we all possess a picture of, a belief about, ourselves which has a significant bearing on our temperament, our personality, our attitudes, etc. In short, your conception of yourself is all-important and practically all your actions and feelings—and your abilities and behavior—are consistent with this self-image.

The concept of self-image, of course, is hardly the property of modern times or of Psycho-Cybernetics alone. The ancient maxim "Know Thyself" is a forerunner of the general approach, which has been broadened by many famous thinkers. In modern days, for example, John Gardner's plea for "Self-renewal" is based on the importance of self-image. Gardner's view is that self-knowledge plus self-esteem (and the discovery of one's potential talent) are the foundation blocks of self-development.

The Psycho-Cybernetic approach revolves around the following pattern: by programming the right kind of feedback to the mind, you can enhance your self-image, which in turn will improve your total behavior.

Self-image, then, is a product of the human brain—a device which we tend to take for granted, but which is a most fantastic mechanism. The brain, of course, controls practically everything we do and its ability to store facts, direct our reasoning, thinking, and physical actions is truly phenomenal. The brain is the forerunner of today's unbelievable computers; indeed, our gray matter is superior to the computer in that it can *create* almost anything. (As a matter of fact, a computer without the benefit of human programming is useless.)

Let's talk about this relationship of the brain and computers just a bit more. The computer industry has the expression "GIGO," which stands for "Garbage In, Garbage Out." What this means is that if your input to the computer is bad, the output is likewise certain to be faulty. It stands to reason that the very same reaction exists in human behavior: direct enough negative input to the brain and the resulting actions are probably going to be "garbage," that is, negative.

While the GIGO process is very obvious, the fact is that most things we assimilate are not black or white; in other words, we may not realize at all that we are piling "garbage" in at any moment—and not realizing this hides from us just why our output (our behavior) is not what it should be or what we would like it to be.

A perfect example of this unrecognized GIGO is proven by the results of hypnotism. No doubt you have seen, or heard about, feats achieved by individuals who have been put into a hypnotic state. They can stand extremes of heat and cold, they can do things physically which in their waking moments they could never dream of doing, their whole personalities can change.

Have you ever wondered why this occurs? Well, to simplify, suffice it to say that the hypnotic state blots out some of the negative input which has limited or restricted the person involved. You can, for example, in fact stand greater heat or cold than you think. What restricts you is the fact that you have been conditioned to pull away from it; remove this conditioned response (through hypnotism, in this case) and your potential for standing extreme temperatures is enhanced. As for physical accomplishments, it has been proven again and again that we tend to develop "contrary muscles" when we have doubts about our abilities; simply by overcoming this mental block we can increase our accomplishments substantially. Lastly, take the case of the "Silent Sam" who, under hypnosis, becomes a babbling idiot; chances are that somewhere in his upbringing he developed a fear (a negative input) of being too loud, too talkative, too boisterous—or something which forced him into a shell; remove this and his "talk potential" increases manyfold.

In a while, I will relate all of this to our subject of making money in stocks, but let me pursue the approach a bit further so that we can develop the method generally and then proceed to our specific motivation for financial gains.

As a result of our brain and our self-image, we as individuals form our own "Comfort Zones" and then tend to live with*in* them. The Comfort Zones, of course, are determined importantly by the amount and degree of the negative (and positive) input we receive and accept. If, for example, you see yourself as weak the chances are that you will only try to accomplish that which is relatively consistent with your self-image. If you stray from this image, you will experience tension (after all, you don't "belong" there and this in itself makes you nervous). And rather than become tense, which in itself encourages failure, you find it more comfortable to return to your "zone" again. Thus, it becomes a vicious circle: the negative input creates the comfort range, the comfort range then determines your potential, and any tension felt once outside that zone merely forms renewed negatives which then confirm and maybe even restrict the range.

None of this is terribly pleasant—*if, that is, your desire is to improve yourself and to get the most from your potential.* Said in five words which should be a motto for us all, "As I think—I AM."

Let me make it clear that I have no intention of making a Walter Mitty out of you. I am not saying that you can be the President of the United States or that you should picture yourself surrounded by a half-dozen Gina Lollobrigidas as a result of your scampering eighty-five yards to win the Big Game in the final four seconds. In other words, there is no need to deceive yourself. But as your data input improves, your self-image is enhanced, and the next thing you know you will begin to act differently (naturally, in an improved way)—in an automatic and spontaneous manner.

Notice the conclusion that your actions will become automatic and spontaneous. Fortunately, the process involved is not arduous; it is not even time-consuming. Instead of requiring a teeth-gritting effort, which is negative itself, the desired changes will become second nature to you.

Enough of the salesmanship, however. No doubt you are wondering just how all this can be accomplished, especially in the quick-and-easy method promised. The answer—the method, that is—lies in the understanding of what is known as *self-talk* and *constructive imagination.*

Now don't run away! In a minute you will see how simple and logical these terms really are.

As for self-talk, it may make you happy to know that you who have been "talking to yourself" all through your life are *not* slated for the "booby hatch." This is a perfectly normal human action. Yes, others talk to themselves, too. What you may not realize is that this self-talk can have a strong bearing on your total behavior in that it is constant data input. Make this input negative enough times and sure enough you will find very negative attitudes forming —fortunately, however, the same is true of positive input and positive attitudes. This self-talk—the words and the thoughts—many times invokes an emotional feeling, which then takes over and rules your reactions. Take the word "mouse." In our earliest years, our first exposures may be to that charming fellow, Mickey, and the thought of mouse probably brings with it a smile, a warm feeling, or something similar. But then we learn that mice evoke "Eeeeks" from men and women alike—that they frighten people and are pesty enough that they have to be trapped. Put another way, our data becomes revised and chances are that our own thoughts and self-talk turn negative relative to these little creatures. The next thing we know, the word "mouse" is converted into an emotional reaction; just as Dr. Pavlov's dog salivated at the hint of being fed, we may feel the kind of squeamish reaction which "Eeeeeek" conditioned. Indeed, it may cause an automatic, spontaneous chill up and down our spines.

The same thing can be said for sounds, smells, images, and all types of thoughts and sensations. Yes, even stock-market thoughts and reactions. As stated, they can be either negative or positive, depending on the data input.

In a minute we will turn to the Psycho-Cybernetic approach and relate it to stock investing. Just to complete the thought, however, let me indicate one way in which normal data input can be altered—in this case, to convert the "Eeeeeek" back to the image of Mickey Mouse.

The Psycho Cybernetic answer lies in the use of "constructive imagination"—a term which pretty much explains itself. It amounts to using your imagination, through self-talk, in a constructive manner. In other words, if you can change the "Eeeeeek" thought to a relaxed warmth or to a humorous reaction or to anything positive, your spontaneous reaction will eventually be positive. If you can form a mental image of mice as pleasant and attractive your potential in this ridiculous area is tremendous. One night you are sitting in a living room with a group of friends and, lo and behold, a mouse appears from nowhere and scampers across the room. Your poor, undisciplined friends leap on to chairs and tables, screeching "Eeeeeek" in all directions and feeling total panic. Not you, though. Your spontaneous reaction is now that mice are pleasant and attractive and you feel this from your agile brain right through your bones. So you sit there, relaxed and happy. Down deep, maybe you even feel an urge to find that poor little creature and pet it. Well, that may be expecting too much!

Despite the example, Psycho-Cybernetics is not to be taken lightly. Through it, your potential for becoming a happier, well-adjusted, more accomplished person is great, simply because of the obliteration of prior negative inputs and the addition of new and constructive ones. Furthermore, an understanding of this approach will develop your ability to understand others. You will enlarge your capacity for *empathy,* which is no more than the ability to see others through *their* mechanisms rather than merely through your own. In other words, once you understand how little bits of negative input can make you into a sort of monster, you will have far greater compassion for others' hangups. Certainly in a competitive game such as the stock market, this capacity to understand others is essential and an important advantage.

Whereas Psycho-Cybernetics can add totally new and positive directions to your life, a different interpretation is necessary for a pursuit such as investing in the stock market. With this in mind, let's now turn to our specific interest and talk about Psycho-Cybernetics and the stock market.

3. Psycho-Cybernetics And The Stock Market

As a securities analyst and manager of money I have been trained to pose both the positives and negatives of any thesis presented to me. In being my own devil's advocate concerning the use of Psycho-Cybernetics within the field of investments, I can see some divergences between the Money Game and an overall approach to living. It is undeniable that our lives can be happier and more successful through more positive thought. But when it comes to a subject which requires some specific information and training, attitude is only one part of the equation. As in the case of the person who strives to be a mathematician, mere constructive imagination of being an accomplished wizard with figures will not make him one. Somewhere along the way he will have to dig in and study and, without this, all the imagination in the world will not convert him into an Einstein or Euclid. By the same token, the investor who experiences significant losses is not going to be helped solely by his own affirmation that he is a successful and happy investor.

In other words, there is a real difference between the use of Psycho-Cybernetics in a business pursuit such as selling a product, where the payoff may be in energy of presentation, hard work, etc., and a field such as investments, where analytical thinking, selection, decision, and action are the crucial elements—and where total success at any moment may be beyond your control.

Thus, in our approach to the stock market we really have two distinct types of data which we have to assemble in order to succeed. The first, like the mathematician, is the specific information and training; and the second, following the Psycho-Cybernetic doctrine, depends on the emotional elements involved. Actually, once we have put the two together, then both Self-Image and our Comfort Zones will have been increased sufficiently so as to lay the groundwork for some really spectacular results.

On the very first page of this book, I emphasized the sad fact that the vast majority of people react incorrectly when it comes to stock investing. Just as ducks take to water and swimming and birds to the air and flying, for some crazy reason—to be corrected herein—human beings drown and flutter and just plain fail to reach their potential in stocks.

Some good part of this failure mechanism can be blamed on the learning input mentioned above; in other words, some people suffer from ignorance—ignorance of the things that go on in the market every day, ignorance of what constitutes a good investment, ignorance of the correct philosophy necessary to accumulate large sums of money. And, yes, even ignorance of where to go to attain the wanted facts or the proper guidance in this all-important subject.

It must be obvious that such ignorance can be overcome. Certainly there is enough written on the subject of stock investing and accumulating fortunes to satisfy anyone's desires. (If this is your situation, let me at least plug my two efforts in this area: *Stock Market Primer* and *The Common Sense Way to Stock Market Profits,* both in hard-cover, published by the World Publishing Company, and in paperback. Both will give you an honest, understandable, and imaginative approach to making money in the stock market.)

Once the ignorance is overcome, however, the would-be successful participant in this exciting and potentially rewarding game has to overcome what is for most an *automatic negative human reaction.*

This reaction is something which I have recognized in myself, something I have seen each and every day of fifteen years in the stock market both through the actions of individuals I have observed and through the mass tendencies of investors generally. Oddly enough, very little has been done to aid people in this area. As many times as stock investing has been treated in publications, the surface of the all-important emotional aspects of investing has barely been scratched.

Here, of course, is where Psycho-Cybernetics comes in.

It stands to reason that the negative human response is due in large part to pure and simple *negative input.* Somewhere along the way, most people have apparently stored input which is decidedly "garbage in." Indeed, those "contrary muscles" we discussed earlier exist relative to stocks; and, as also mentioned, the Comfort Zone of most investors has become one of mediocre-to-poor performance, which in itself restricts future possibilities. In computer terminology, garbage in leads inevitably to garbage out.

What, then, can we do to change this?

The answer lies in understanding the negative input and in replacing this with positive and constructive data.

My approach to this has been:

1. To analyze the *right* way to do things, to deduce from this what most people seem to be lacking—and to determine what kind of negative input might be blocking out proper thoughts and actions; and

2. To analyze what I have observed investors repeatedly doing *wrong* and explore just why they repeat such incorrect procedure—once again attempting to isolate any negative input which appears to be responsible for such actions.

The result will be a substitution of constructive, positive, and practical data in place of the restrictive and negative—all of which will go a long way towards making you the kind of intuitive investor who reacts wisely in his decisions. Equally important, you should become more relaxed and just plain happier in your investment life. Believe me, this serenity is worth many, many dollars.

The chapters to follow take a buckshot approach to the most important data. Needless to say, you are not going to be hit where it hurts everywhere. This does not mean that you should pass over those which do not apply personally. Bits of valuable general advice are contained throughout. Furthermore, as mentioned in the previous chapter, your ability to comprehend why others behave as they do, and your increased empathy make you more sophisticated and more competitive in stock-market investing. For stock prices reflect what people *think* given companies are worth, and such thinking is naturally affected by all types of emotional tendencies. Thus the person who understands crowd actions which so often take over the market has a distinct advantage over those who do not. The person who understands hope, greed, and fear—which constitute the basis for most investment reactions—has the upper hand over those who simply act, without knowing why. Lastly, the individual who "knows himself" has a far better chance for success in general, which includes the all-important peace of mind already stressed as an essential in one's quest for dollars.

Fortunately, much of what follows relates to more than the stock market. You will find examples which point up inputs having a bearing on business in general, sports, the family, gambling, and a host of personality and temperament adjustments we should all at least consider. I trust the reading will have general entertainment value as well as providing improved attitudes towards both investing and life in general.

4. Back To The Womb—Or How Not To Approach Life Or The Stock Market

It goes without saying that we humans are a strange bunch. Walk down the street and observe the people around you—or go where larger numbers of people congregate. Did you ever see such an assortment of faces in your life? All with two eyes, a nose, a mouth, two ears—but in the damnedest combinations imaginable. And, you know, there's a temperament and personality which fits each of those countenances.

Naturally, human beings do have certain common characteristics—but once again these show sharp variation. If I were to ask you what characteristics are most common, what would you answer? The need simply to exist? The desire to be happy? The urge for some sort of companionship? The need for security?

All these are legitimate and practical answers, but I wonder how many of you would have thought to include one of the most consistent and most significant of all: *the feeling of inferiority.*

I'll bet I know your reaction to this last statement. It probably goes something like: "Well, that's true about me, but it certainly doesn't go for that obnoxious Herkimer Gladpimple down at the office, or for most of the people I know." If that is your reaction, you will be amazed to know what psychological studies on the subject have shown. Some take the extreme position that there is no such thing as a superiority complex at all—that any person who exhibits this is merely trying to cover up for his basic feeling of inferiority. Whether or not that is true has no real bearing on the point here. What is important is the realization that *practically everyone suffers in some way from inferiority feelings and that this hampers your potential more than you can imagine.* In Dr. Maltz's book, *Psycho-Cybernetics,* the statement is made: "At least 95 percent of the people have their lives blighted by feelings of inferiority to some extent, and to millions this same feeling of inferiority is a serious handicap to success and happiness."

Whenever I think of people who lack real confidence and don't choose to do anything about it, the expression used in the title of this chapter comes to my mind. It's like the following pathetic character

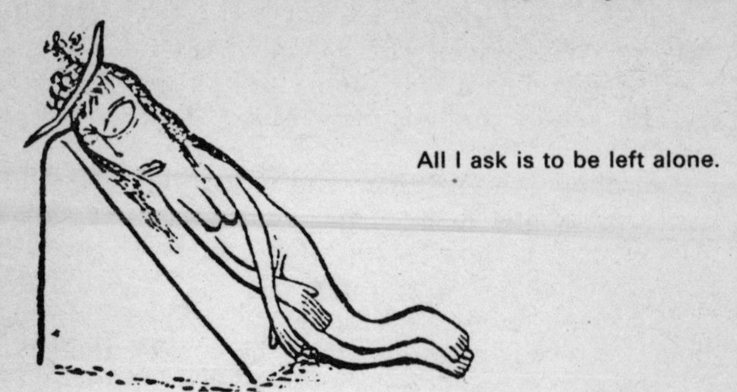
All I ask is to be left alone.

done by the famous cartoonist, William Steig. She is obviously feeling very sorry for herself and is suffering from exposure to the outside world. The poor thing is pleading to escape "back to the womb," which is neither possible nor commendable.

No, the solution is to to do something positive, which involves moving further away from the womb —and overcoming as much as possible those feelings of inferiority which really restrict progress and happiness.

Enough of this, however. What bearing does this have on successful stock-market investing?

Well, just for openers, it is obvious to me that *a huge percentage of investors suffer from a stock-market inferiority complex.* A discussion of why this exists could well develop into a "chicken-and-egg" argument, as one might ask whether the complex exists because so many have failed over the years or whether an original feeling of inferiority is what in fact led to such failure. Actually, both are valid—and both are phenomena I plan to correct.

While it is not my place to pose all the complicated reasons behind emotional hangups, one definite source of no confidence stems from a tendency on the part of many to shoot for perfection and thus to be shattered when they are unable to achieve their goals, which were unrealistic to begin with. Who, for example, consistently buys at the very bottom and sells at the very top? Nobody! But if you set this up as your goal, you are in for constant disappointment—which may develop into a feeling of inferiority. If you sell a stock at fifty dollars and expect it to decline from there immediately (or even eventually), you have made a goal which is certain to prove unachievable. Thus, the failure to achieve perfection *does not spell failure at all.*

Actually, people have this uncertain, insecure feeling about all types of investments. If you don't believe this, consider for a moment the billions and billions of dollars which today (and in the past) have languished in unproductive savings accounts of all sorts. Take the case of July, 1970. Despite the fact that "riskless" short-term government securities (Treasury bills and notes) provided returns of 8 to 9 percent, some $420 billions rested in bank and savings and loan accounts drawing a paltry 4 to 5 percent. While to some extent this anomaly is due to procrastination or laziness or lack of knowledge—and while some is due to the fact that a certain amount of emergency, "rainy-day" money is involved—the logical explanation is that the depositors' decisions emanate in large degree from a massive sense of insecurity and lack of confidence.

Carrying this one important step further, what kind of common-stock investor do you suppose such a person is who doesn't avail himself of this kind of significantly higher return? My experience has shown me that he is generally not the best. He can eventually be, but he has to overcome a feeling of insecurity and any number of fears first.

As suggested, lack of knowledge can contribute significantly to this malady. There is a human tendency to fear the unknown—and to become nervous when we know down deep that we are relatively ignorant of the crucial facts. The pages to follow will overcome both the ignorance and fear which are sources of investment mediocrity.

Thus, if you are one who has sat idly by with a lot of money not working adequately you may need the kind of altered approach which an investor I know finally developed. This person—let's call him Mr. Sit-tight—came to see me one day. He presented me with a list of securities which had done little for him over the years and which was about as interesting as yesterday's laundry. When I quizzed him about his objectives and about his overall position, he finally 'fessed up to the fact that he had, in addition, some $300,000 scattered in thirty different bank savings accounts. All were drawing interest of 3 to 4 percent. "No wonder," I thought, "he has failed to succeed with his list of common stocks. He has taken the same, insecure approach to these that he has to his savings dollars."

Just how and what we accomplished from this point is interesting—and relative to this discussion. First of all, I could see that Mr. Sit-tight was suffering from a severe inferiority complex, which I felt could be approached better through bolstering his income than from trying to convince him that the way to investment success is through achievement of capital gains. After all, *people should be happy with their investments and should not be placed into positions of stress.*

At any rate, I suggested switching nearly all the $300,000 out of savings banks and into *short-term* government bonds which yielded approximately 6 percent. This immediately raised his income on this sum from around $10,000 per year to $18,000. At the same time I suggested that he "clean house" in his stock list by eliminating the weaker equities, most of which were held by him only because of their dividends. With the proceeds I constructed a portfolio of fine growth companies, including IBM, Xerox, Johnson & Johnson, American Home Products, Merck, 3M, Eastman Kodak, Coca-Cola, American Express, and Hewlett-Packard. These stocks also totaled around $300,000 and provided dividends of approximately $6,000 per year—which was $6,000 less than he had been collecting on this segment of his investments. Overall, therefore, he added $8,000 in annual income from the fixed-income portion (the bonds) and reduced $6,000 from the equity (stock) segment —for a net addition of $2,000.

While the combination of higher returns plus the wisdom of owning growth stocks should have brought a sparkle to his eyes, his reaction was one of uncertainty. He left my office, not yet shaken from his ingrained sense of insecurity, to think it over. Some years later he confessed to me the battle which took place in his mind over the following few days. Indeed, it was a struggle between back-to-the-womb and breaking out. Fortunately, the latter prevailed, because within a few years the $300,000 in growth stocks had appreciated to almost a half-million and the rising dividends from these companies had hiked his admittedly small income from this source by over 30 percent.

Interestingly enough, Mr. Sit-tight's real risks (to be discussed in chapter 7) were actually less after the changes than before. Most important, he was converted from an unknowing, insecure, do-nothing investor to a more confident doer.

This story should make you realize that there is little to be gained from a back-to-the-womb approach. You, like Mr. Sit-tight, may have to engage in some extensive self-talk in order to enlarge your Comfort Zone, but like him you have the same potential for success. *Remember that do-nothing dollars achieve do-nothing results.* Remember also, however, that the key to action is in *proper* action. Substituting low-grade securities for bank accounts is hardly the answer.

The Huddling Instinct—A Way Not to Compensate for Insecurity

Another part of the insecurity syndrome has to do with a tendency to huddle with the crowd and to do what others are doing. How hard it is for an individual to sell his Westinghouse when he knows that others are optimistic. How difficult it is for a portfolio manager of a large mutual fund to let his Boise Cascade go when he knows that his competitors are holding the same stock. A strong *fear of missing the boat* is responsible for the natural instinct to huddle.

Yes, the easy way out is to conform. But that is not the right way to achieve good investment results over the years. Later on I will explain just when it is best to be contrary and when there is wisdom in some conformity, but for the moment it is more important to understand the human tendency to follow established trends and, instead, to learn how to buck them.

One excellent way is to remind yourself of the simple fact that the masses are almost always wrong. Whether you follow the history of fads and sudden popularities or whether you know that the so-called odd-lotters in the stock market have proved themselves wrong consistently, the facts are irrefutable. People follow the paths of least resistance and, when it comes to investments, end up with little to show for it.

A deeper and more significant factor to consider has to do with *supply and demand.* Stock prices are naturally the result of such supply-and-demand relationships. When supply of shares is heavy in relation to demand, prices go down; and when supply is dried up and demand is strong, values go skyrocketing.

So—ask yourself the question: what does conformity mean in terms of supply and demand? The answer: *conformity means excess.* Thus, if people are all optimistic about Westinghouse, this creates unusual demand for the stock; and unless there is some abnormal supply to offset this, the price rises as a result. Carrying the reasoning one step further, *the huddling instinct means that the huddler comes in when the supply-demand balance is already out of whack.*

Therefore, while conforming may give the conformist a sense of security, in fact he is falling into a trap. There is great wisdom in *not* accepting or going by appearances of what may seem to promise serenity. There is no safety in numbers when the numbers have already had their effect on supply and demand. Indeed, the odds are actually stacked against you.

False Security from the "Comfort" of Dividends

Cash dividends, lovely though they may be to receive, can lull a stockholder into a false sense of security about his investments—and can lead to a refusal to assess things realistically. How many times, for example, have I observed investors deceiving themselves about their poor choices through the rationale that the dividend income has remained intact. I'm sure that many thousands of American Telephone shareholders have justified their investment this way. Whereas the cash payout on 100 shares of Ma Bell increased from $180 per year in 1962 to $240 in 1970, the same 100 shares depreciated in value by a couple of thousand dollars. Thus, Telephone has hardly been an ideal investment, and the least a person should do is to question why the loss has occurred.

In many cases, furthermore, dividends have not advanced as did Telephone's—and yet investors tend to go through the same deceptive thought process. "Oh well, they keep paying their dividends" is simply an escape from an unpleasant reality. Another is "Well, the stock now yields 8 percent—and that's darned high." What this person may fail to consider is that the dividend may be narrowly covered by earnings, which means that a reduction may be just around the corner.

And then there is the more unusual case in which *hidden* consequences exist—like that of the former Kern County Land Company (now part of Tenneco). Kern County Land's problem was not one of declining market value; as a matter of fact, the stock had increased slightly over the period from 1958 to 1966, and it had paid out a healthy dividend during each of those years. Not that this was a satisfactory performance; it was not, as other stocks over the same span had done famously. But at least some capital appreciation occurred. The trouble was that KCL was basically an asset company—with oil constituting the major holding—and the company was not replacing its assets as they were withdrawn. In other words, since oil does not reproduce itself, if you extract it and do not somehow add to your reserves, you will ultimately run out of your precious commodity. Many KCL shareholders were deceived by the steady and large dividends being paid to them, whereas in effect these dividends were being paid out of a diminishing asset. Had the company been able to replace its oil through comparable newly found reserves, or through other potential sources of earning power, then this criticism would not be valid, but for many years this was not the case.

Incidentally, the tax consequences of the KCL-type situation involve a further negative in that the dividend was taxable at ordinary income rates instead of what might have been defined as return of capital—which would have carried a lower, capital-gains levy.

At any rate, too many investors hide behind the cloak of security which dividends often provide and, as a result, refuse to see their investments for what they truly are. Dividends are, of course, totally dependent on earnings, which means that they (dividends) should be relegated to their true secondary position. While high dividends may provide some kind of "floor" for a stock, in most cases this simply results from paying out a higher portion of earnings than do others. High payout itself may be a sign of weakness, as one would like to think that his company would choose to reinvest substantial sums towards significant growth, rather than pay most of it out. Lastly, dividends can be dwarfed in no time by market performance; when you consider the fact that very high yields on stocks amount to only 7 or 8 percent, such returns can be seen to be but a drop in the bucket compared to potential capital gains or losses.

Advice for Those Who Are "There"

An adjunct to this discussion has to do with those who are no longer planning for the distant future because they are already at or near the point of retirement. This, of course, is when a secure attitude is most crucial. For the person who has waited too long and who has not provided for himself in the proper way, I can be of little help. However, I can address myself to the multitude of older people who complain that they lack resources to live the way they want to, but who really do have sufficient funds. So now we turn to the delicate subject of spending capital.

Years ago, when interest rates were extremely low, I used to hear a constant complaint from people who had large sums like $100,000, $200,000, $300,-000, $400,000, or even half a million. With yields at that time (in a combined bond and stock portfolio) averaging 3 to 5 percent, this meant that investment income would range from $3,000 to $5,000 per year for the $100,000 list to "only" $15,000 to $25,000 for the half-million-dollar portfolio. Since many were retiring from jobs which paid a good deal more than these income figures, you can understand why some felt strapped. And correspondingly, I might add, insecure. And envious.

The answer, to my way of thinking, lay in the spending of capital—something which I found to be abhorrent to most people. Not that I recommended huge chunks being turned to daily living needs. It would be foolhardy to plan on drawing $10,000 per year out of a nest egg of $100,000; this combined with a severe market decline would place such spenders in danger of the poorhouse. But a few thousand here and a few thousand there made total sense. After all, capital has limited utility when it is hoarded. Although my plan was logical, it took some talking to convince most people that this was the prudent and sensible road to follow.

While 1970 brought with it a different return pattern—i.e., much higher dividends and interest rates—the cost of living has risen too, and either you or your older relatives may be facing similar capital decisions. Once again, the emotions of insecurity and the fear of poverty (to be discussed later) may combine to restrict a person from doing what is right.

Thus, the explanation of such emotional reactions should lay the groundwork for the proper approach and frame of mind. Whether you are investing for the future or living for today, happiness and security are interrelated—something which I hope has been placed in proper perspective. Remember, there are plenty of happy poor people in this world—and too darned many unhappy rich ones. *Psycho-Cybernetics and the Stock Market* aims to enrich all groups, both financially and emotionally.

How to Become "Correctly Parental" with Your Stocks

As long as we are on the subject of mother, security, and insecurity, let's talk about the parental tendency which investors display about the stocks they own. Like some ordinary mommies and daddies, there are people who refuse to believe anything but the best of their "offspring"; needless to say, this lack of realism is hardly conducive to the continuous assessment and objective appraisal which is necessary in the upbringing of an investment.

Another kind of behavior is shown by those investors who tend to become downright deserters. Instead of understanding the needs of their "children," they wear blinkers to everything around them and end up paying no attention to something which requires plenty of thought and consideration.

Still other stockholders go so far as to fall in love with their inanimate little stocks just as though they were alive, and behave accordingly. For example, I have heard hundreds of people say that the very thought of selling a particular security is like "taking a piece out of me."

The derivations of these thought patterns are obviously diverse. Some might evolve from a sense of loyalty towards one's possessions; some might be the product of the human tendency to become and stay a creature of habit. And some might be influenced by what I term the "Xerox Complex"—the constant fear that something they sell today will become the Xerox of tomorrow.

Whereas parenthood of flesh-and-blood children should foster relationships lasting a lifetime, such is definitely *not* the case when it comes to stocks. As a matter of fact, it is my contention that over 90 percent of the securities available for investment in the public market are anything but potential lifetime possessions. This may shock you—and it may seem especially startling coming from a person who is opposed (as I am) to in-and-out trading or any hint of excessive activity on the part of investors. The fact is, however, that a very high percentage of stocks are cyclical in some way. They may be so because they are sensitive to the general economy—which is bound to experience its ups and downs. Or they may be subject to cycles of their own, due probably to some temporary imbalance of supply and demand within their industry. Or they may be cyclical simply because the human beings who are the daily "voters" within the stock market tend towards ridiculous extremes of optimism and pessimism and simply create prices which are out of line with reality. Later on, I will distinguish those areas which plead for extra patience from those just described, which require very close surveillance. In general, however, you should recognize the fact that stocks demand some parental coddling. Like human offspring, each requires some slightly different treatment. For the moment, accept the generalizations that stocks do not grow to be strong and healthy investments if they are surrounded by permissive, "can't do wrong" love, or if they are guided by nervousness.

Indeed, there is a happy medium—something which can be reached through an understanding of what is to follow here. As already mentioned, a combination of common-sense investment philosophy plus an understanding of the all-important emotional factors involved in the ownership of stocks should achieve this happy middle position. That is what Correct Parenthood within the stock market is all about.

5. The Stock Market: Mysterious Or Not?

I'd like to have a nickel for each time I have heard a remark like "The stock market is a mystery to me" or "Gad, what a complicated thing the market is." I imagine something like this is uttered a couple of hundred thousand times a day—maybe even a few million—as interested people leaf through the financial pages and note the pluses and minuses which mark movements in the stock market.

Indirectly, those showing such negative thought patterns are fostering the very insecurity-inferiority complexes already discussed as detrimental to one's progress. In other words, the guy who goes around saying (or just thinking) that the stock market is a mystery is stacking the chips against himself right from the start.

So, the first negative input we want to eliminate is the thought that the market is impossible or even very difficult to comprehend.

Quite honestly I think I can convince you that investing in stocks need not be terribly complicated. As a matter of fact, most individuals make such investing far more difficult than it need be. This plus the restrictive emotional reactions we are discussing in this book combine to confuse the issue. In short, humans are inclined to seek scapegoats for failures for which they themselves are to blame; and it is my strong belief that too many blame the stock market itself for their own negligence in not taking the proper time and thought in approaching it.

The Black-and-White Thinker

One victim of "The stock market is a mystery" hangup is the person who thinks mainly in terms of absolutes and who therefore expects things to be either one way or the other. The individual, for example, who views the market as being always in either a bull or a bear condition is one who leaves himself open to frustration. When he concludes that a bull market is in progress he is bound to expect exciting profits for himself; anything short of this leads to a questioning of either his own abilities or his broker's or it casts doubts on the whole system. At the other extreme—a bear market—such a person expects only declining values—and this expectation obliterates even the possibility of what might be a more sensible optimism.Both these extremes, therefore, foster constant nervousness—certainly not the ideal input for the well-adjusted investor. Furthermore, such polarization tends to promote the greed and fear which are responsible for the worst problems in the stock market.

Whereas one cannot escape the labeling of bull and bear markets by others, investments are best viewed in an atmosphere which is not so definitely black and white. Consider how many groups of industries have failed to participate in the overall good markets of recent years—e.g., steels, chemicals, foods, utilities, natural gas, railroads, etc. By the same token, remember that many individual and group stars blossom during the depths of the very worst bear markets.

Thus, it is usually best to view investments in a less emotional framework—one which does not literally breed anxieties, as this absolute and extreme thinking does. If one's expectations are not exaggerated, there is a logical and more relaxed approach which can produce extremely worthwhile results.

A Non-Mysterious Approach

All of this certainly places on me the onus of indicating just how the market can be tackled without an arduous effort—which I believe it can. The answer lies in little more than owning decent companies which are engaged in attractive industries and paying prices for such ownership which are not drastically out of line with prospects for the future.

No—I am not putting you on. There is not one iota of facetiousness in this statement. I reiterate that there is no great trick to finding decent companies operating in good industries without having to pay through the nose. The trouble with most people—and I include stock analysts, stockbrokers, and most professional money managers alike—is that *they lack discipline of any kind in their approach to investments*. They run helter skelter through the berry patch, losing sight of the fact that, with proper consideration, a relaxed stroll will fill their baskets much earlier and fuller.

The proper disciplines are those which I have emphasized in my previous books; they refer mainly to industry prospects and industry position. Rather than look for a pig in a poke, you can build yourself a very attractive portfolio of stocks if you set your mind to:

1. Investing in industries which are by no means mature and which possess demand patterns which guarantee their above-average growth for many years to come.
2. Within the definition just given, confining yourself to those fields which have not suddenly attracted a raft of competition.
3. Concentrating on industries which are not so sensitive to the business cycle that their business will fluctuate sharply during the inevitable ups and downs which will occur in any economy.

4. Involving yourself in industries which have low labor content.

5. Emphasizing groups which have the ability to increase their product prices consistently and which do not produce a diminution of demand because of these higher prices.

Given the right company within this framework the need for precise timing of purchases and the need for constant selling of your securities become *relatively* minor matters. Granted that this is a simplification of the total procedure, I have found that the approach:

1. Will seldom get you in trouble;
2. Will point you to the most attractive areas for investment over the years; and
3. Will force you into a frame of mind which will provide:
   a. the confidence we all need to succeed;
   b. the kind of investment philosophy which by itself will overcome those restrictive human reactions we have discussed;
   c. the scope and patience which are essential to achieving the ultimate possibilities with your investments.

So much for the generalities, however. It is one thing to understand ideal characteristics and it is another to know just which industries fit into which category. Stated another way, if there were only a way by which a person could assess the basic industries for their overall strengths and weaknesses, stock investing would lose most of its mystery.

In a minute I will provide you with my assessment of industry strengths—something which, believe it or not, will take very little space and an insignificant amount of your time to utilize. I have presented just such an industry categorization in my two previous books; these have appeared over the last nine years and I am pleased to see that they have weathered the storms of time and have led those using them to the right areas for investment.

Let me make it clear that I do not hold myself out to be expert on all industries. It is no great trick, however, to assess *relative* strengths—which is all we are trying to accomplish. Most important, this approach sets out *disciplines* which keep people from stabbing in the dark and which simplify the job of stock selection.

On pages 57–58 you will find my Industry Strength Guide. As you will see, I have first divided the industries available for investment in today's market into three groups:

1. Those directly sensitive to the overall business cycle;
2. Those with cyclical tendencies of their own (not necessarily in line with that of the general economy); and
3. Those pretty much impervious to general business conditions, which have either strong enough demand patterns or some special characteristics which enable them to resist such cycles.

Within each of these three groupings, I have rated the industries based mainly on the points stressed on pages 52–53. In doing so, I have assigned the ratings on a scale, with 1 given to the very strongest industries on down to 4 for the weakest.

Now see just how difficult and mysterious the stock market is! Day in and day out your best opportunities will exist in stocks of the third (noncyclical) category that are rated 1 and 2. Finding strong, well-managed companies within these fields will not be difficult and your job really consists of selecting them and seeing to it that your price of entry is not out of line with normal growth rates.

This is not to say that money is to be made solely from noncyclical stocks. The noncyclicals do not require as much attention or as much flexibility on the part of their owners, but significant opportunities exist elsewhere and you should certainly consider them too. Going beyond the noncyclical category requires that you try to gauge the approximate stage of the cycle in question and then to act according to your assessment, consciously reminding yourself that you must expect erratic behavior from the stock and that you therefore must buy at the troughs and sell at the peaks if you are to achieve a decent rate of return on your investment. (Note: cyclical stocks, in my opinion, have really not been adequately discussed in textbooks and other writings; if this subject interests you, I strongly suggest you read chapters 7, 19, and 21 of my book, *The Common Sense Way to Stock Market Profits.*) At any rate, we will cover the best approach to this kind of money-making in chapter 17.

To emphasize the point made here, let me make an analogy with the technique of a successful builder. Through an understanding of industry strength, you have managed to find the best location for your new "building." You have only to choose the right kind of building (i.e., the right kind of company operating within this attractive field) and to erect it at a cost (pay a price for the stock) which promises a decent return on your dollars over the years.

Later I will discuss in detail the matter of price. For the moment, however, let's agree that the stock market does not have to be a mystery. Quite the contrary! By knowing that your approach to investing is logical and well disciplined, you will eliminate the negative input of belief that the stock market is mysterious.

Let me repeat that I do not pose as an expert on all industries. You or your investment adviser should work out your own model, which may well differ from mine. I doubt that it will differ significantly from mine, however, as what we are assessing is *basic* strength—industry position *over a long period of time.* As will be explained fully in chapter 17, practically every industry group experiences occasional deviations from the norm. The important consideration, therefore, is *to know the real reason that you own what you do.* For example, you may take a position in automobiles because you see great demand for them coming up, and you may make considerable money from them. To make the maximum, however, you must not forget that autos *are* cyclical—which indicates that you will have to sell before the cycle turns downward. Or you may see the food issues as attractive—but you should not lose sight of the fact (at least in my assessment, as shown in the Industry Strength Guide) that this group has below-average basic strength. Therefore, if your investment objec-

INDUSTRY STRENGTH GUIDE

CATEGORY I: INDUSTRIES DIRECTLY SENSITIVE TO GENERAL BUSINESS CYCLE

Ratings

1	2	3	4
Rubber	Aluminum	Auto parts	Lead, zinc
	Automotive	Copper	Railroads (without other income)
	Chemicals	Radio & TV	Trucking
	Containers	Railroads (with other income)	
	Fiberglass	Steel	
	Paper		
	Retail trade		

CATEGORY II: INDUSTRIES WITH CYCLICAL TENDENCIES OF THEIR OWN

Ratings

1	2	3	4
Electrical equipment	Airlines	Building materials	Aerospace
Electronics	Air conditioning	Cement	Rail equipment (construction)
	Broadcasting	Containers	Shipbuilding
	Coal	Farm equipment	
	Construction equipment	Food chains	
	Forest products (integrated)	Insurance (property)	
	Hotels	LPG distributors	
	Mobile homes	Motion pictures	
	Newspapers	Petroleum (refiners)	
	Offshore drilling	Printing	
	Semiconductors	Restaurant chains	
		Savings & loan	
		Textiles	

CATEGORY III: INDUSTRIES WITHOUT CYCLICAL TENDENCIES

Ratings

1	2	3	4
Computers (IBM)	Computers (ex-IBM)	Banks	Finance companies
Cosmetics	Computer peripheral	Beer	Tobacco
Drugs (proprietary)	Drugs (ethical)	Computer software	
		Distilling	

CATEGORY III: INDUSTRIES WITHOUT CYCLICAL TENDENCIES
(*continued*)

Ratings			
1	2	3	4
Hospital products	Household products	Electrical utilities	
Office equipment	Leisure-time	Foods	
Photography	Life insurance	Hospitals	
Services	Specialty retailing	Natural gas	
Soft drinks		Petroleum (integrated)	
		Petroleum (producers)	
		Publishing	
		Rail car leasing	
		Telephone	

tive to high growth, you must not deceive yourself into believing that food stocks will provide such results over an extended period of time.

Thus, *a temporary gain does not spell long-term victory* and it is essential not to let near-term success obliterate good judgment. People tend to fall in love with their ideas to the point of losing objectivity—a habit which must be corrected. Like any top strategist, your game plan must be thought out, clearly understood, and then followed rationally (not emotionally).

Obviously, the Industry Strength Guide does not allow for the vast differences among the various companies within each industry. Despite this, assessment of relative group strengths constitutes an excellent and necessary starting point from which other decisions can be made. Most important, this approach emphasizes the *disciplines* which keep people from wandering aimlessly, which simplify the job of stock selection, and which bolster the ability to sell stocks at high prices. All of this will be tied together for you in chapter 19.

The Successful Failure—Or Why Do Prosperous Businessmen So Often Fail in the Market

One factor contributing to the market's image of mystery is the failure experienced by so many people who are successful in other pursuits. Now for the doctor or dentist or the butcher, baker, or electrician,* this may not seem so incongruous since business training and an understanding of economics has not been an integral part of their occupational success. But when the businessman himself continuously goes down to defeat—which he often does—then the nonmystery argument may seem flimsy.

Shortly after I entered the securities business —in the mid-1950s—I met just such a man, that is, one who had been quite successful in his own business and yet had been a total failure in his stock investing.

Not much later I encountered another individual who also had followed this pattern. Here was a fellow who had started a business from scratch, built it into something entirely unique, and made it so profitable that he was able to sell it to a major company for a few million dollars. And how was he doing with these dollars in the stock market? In a word: terribly!

And then I met another person who had the same experience.

And then another.

Until I finally discovered that the apparent in-

*Candlesticks replaced by light bulbs.

consistency was not unusual at all. Instead, it was fairly typical.

This interested me, and I set out to analyze why it should happen. After all, a person who proves himself in business should find many similarities between that and the market.

The results of my study are meaningful to *every* potential investor, so let's explore them.

To begin with, I discovered that these individuals lacked the basic philosophy and disciplines stressed thus far. In some cases this was because they were extremely busy in their everyday pursuits and refused to take even the small amount of time necessary to develop a common-sense approach.

In many cases, however, failure did not stem from lack of time. In some it was an example of overreaching—a case of assuming that because they had made it in one area, anything remotely related should come easily. Contributing to this misapprehension was the idea that they could transfer the "gut feel" which they had developed in their own business to the specialty of picking stocks. Thus, they had become accustomed to seat-of-the-pants, intuitive decisions in their own area and simply applied the identical approach to the market—with which they had little or no experience, knowledge, or discipline. Proper inputs had been responsible for the formation of intuition in their specialized field—inputs which were either lacking or negative insofar as the stock market was concerned. Thus, even these success-oriented businessmen suffered from emotional hangups which restricted proper investment technique. Alas, a human being is a human being is a human being, and the need for an altered psychological framework was as strong with them as with others.

Lastly, many of these business-success–market-failures were unwilling to listen, as they should have. Too many of this group refused to recognize or seek-out the expertise of a market specialist and took on the market as a personal challenge. Humility is a great human trait and one should not let success in one area prevent one from having an open mind in another area.

I could now skirt the issue by making the bold statement that the key to successful money management is to find an individual who is a keen student of his profession and who is accomplished in stock selection—and then to give him his head. While the theory is sound enough, it breaks down simply because investors experience difficulty in finding a broker or a counselor in whom they have complete confidence. Whether it be the billions of dollars managed by mutual funds or comparable amounts under direction of individual counselors and brokers, investing is more an art than a science and it is more difficult to generate confidence in such artists than it is in your family dentist—who can solve the problem of pain through extracting the abscessed tooth or replacing the decayed area with metal.

"The Trouble with Harry"

Psycho-Cybernetics and the Stock Market deals with the problems of everyone and anyone handling and investing money, whether it be a mutual-fund manager, a portfolio manager for a large insurance company or similar institution, an investment adviser, a broker, or anyone owning stock. While many individuals solve the problem of making decisions by buying mutual funds and the like, many do not choose this route and instead work closely with brokers. And here is where some real hangups come to light—which prompts me to bring up the subject of brokers and *their* problems (*which ultimately become the problems of their clients*).

It is true that brokers are far better trained today than at any time in the past—and that most firms have more extensive research facilities than ever before. Unfortunately, neither training nor research ensure against losses, nor will they ever.

At the risk of incurring the wrath of the various stock exchanges, as well as brokers generally, there are some natural conflicts of interest inherent in a situation in which the generation of commissions constitutes the basis for one's income. Let's face it, brokers are in business to do business, and it takes exceptional people to put your best interests ahead of their livelihood. That is, it may be better for the investor to hold certain stocks for many years and to avoid selling them and yet to do so would hardly be beneficial to the broker's income statement. Equally unbeneficial to the broker are those times when people should sit with cash and not invest in much of anything. Then too, there is the broker who is an investment banker and who must raise money for certain corporations. There are bound to be occasions when what is good for the corporation client may be at best marginally beneficial to the investor client (and sometimes, to be blunt, may even be to the disadvantage of the investor).

These negatives do not preclude a good job being done for the investor; they simply tend to inhibit performance. Thus, with stocks, as with so many other business-customer relationships, it is a matter of *caveat emptor* (let the buyer beware).

In seeking out the right broker, I stress the following characteristics:

1. Obvious honesty and integrity, which might be boiled down to "The client's interest always comes first."

2. A knowledge of the business in depth. This means having a broker who is more than a "story buyer" and who understands something about industry strengths, basic characteristics, etc.

3. A person who comprehends risks and who can give you a good idea of the risk you are taking in anything you buy.

4. An individual with sufficient imagination to bring more than run-of-the-mill results (which we have already defined as basically poor).

5. A person with strong discipline which shapes his approach to the market and stock selection.

6. A person who goes beyond merely pushing stocks on you and who instead recognizes the importance of structuring your investments (to be explained in chapter 21).

7. An individual with decent judgment—and one whose "investment personality" complements yours (chapter 14 will provide a questionnaire designed to aid you in accomplishing this).

8. Someone who comprehends the psychological aspects of investing, both as related to you, to

himself, and to the mass movements which are a product of people in general.

Perhaps you will have difficulty finding this ideal individual. While you cannot expect him to have the batting average of your doctor or lawyer or accountant, he does exist—and you should at least strive to find someone with as many of these qualities as you can. In any case, this book is geared to cover the basics of the knowledge, risks, imagination, discipline, judgment, and psychology emphasized above.

Conclusions

Back to our chapter's thesis, the stock market itself is not a culprit. Nor need it be mysterious. A rational approach plus some rational behavior plus some rational advice can convert any individual or any group from also-rans to winners.

The sensible approach, therefore, is to:

1. Understand your investment in terms of industry characteristics and its individual strengths and weaknesses;
2. Pay a realistic price;
3. Maintain a disciplined attitude as to the time to sell; and
4. Use great care in selecting an adviser or broker on whom you may rely for information and advice.

6. Eliot Ness Not Needed

While we're on the subject of mystery let me explore one little misconception which has been responsible for some negative input on the part of many investors.

I am referring to something which is a hangover from the days—many years ago—when stock pools and other manipulative practices existed in the stock market. At that time many people developed the habit of attributing responsibility for everyday market activity to these secret groups. I suppose, at the beginning, the talkers said something like, "Well, the 'pool' bid them up today" or "The 'group' sold stocks like they were going out of style" or something similar. In time, reference to the "pool" or "group" changed simply to "they," and suddenly "they" took on the connotation of collusion and other unpleasantness.

Despite the fact that the stock market has come under very stringent regulations, with the elimination of pools and such out-to-fleece-the-public organizations, the habit of referring to "they" has been passed down and still exists today. And the meaning behind its use is still decidedly negative—as if there are groups of Big Bad Wolves constantly stalking a prey of innocent Grandmas and Little Red Riding Hoods and devouring them by the minute on the floor of the exchange.

Now don't think me naïve. I am not arguing that all is lily-white when it comes to stocks and the marketplace. In addition, I should point out that a group of so-called traders still exists on the floor of the exchanges—persons who earn their living by going in and out of stocks on a regular basis, sometimes holding positions for only minutes. Actually these traders, plus the exchange "specialists," serve the function of providing liquidity to stocks when investors don't do so; and there are plenty of times when they lose sizable sums in the process. If, however, your approach to making money in stocks is similar to that of the traders in that you plan to be extremely active and make a multitude of small, short-term coups, then you should know that these fellows are very formidable competition. The fact that those on the floor can trade without paying commissions (their ownership of seats on the exchange entitles them to this privilege) certainly places you at a competitive disadvantage. In this case, you might not be criticized for pointing your finger to a "they."

But, to my way of thinking, anyone who plans to prosper in stocks through day-to-day trading activity is totally foolish and ill-advised to begin with. What I am saying, therefore, is that there is no "they" facing a pure investor. Even if someone does take you for an occasional one-eighth or one-quarter of a point, it will have minute bearing on your success. Your approach should be to try and make consistent and man-sized returns on your dollars, and the traders are not going to have an effect on this kind of prosperity.

The modern-day version of the "they" gremlins of the 1920s must be the mutual funds and other large investors of the late 1960s who, by virtue of their size, hold a power which parallels the pools of the earlier era. Many smaller investors have expressed fears over how these institutions can control stock prices and how they (the smaller investors) have been taken financial advantage of by them.

Fortunately for the worriers about "they" and unfortunately for the owners of these large funds, the stock-market experience of 1969 and early 1970 has demonstrated that no privileged group has succeeded to the detriment of others. The human frailties of even the most sophisticated institutional money and its managers came out in the open—with very disappointing performance results for the period. The performance game has become extremely competitive and actions of one large fund have apparently offset the contrary actions of another. To be more specific, investment results of 1969 and 1970 were sufficiently disappointing to allay any fears that combined groups were able to succeed at the expense of the "little man." Indeed, small size alone can be a form of protection. Except for very occasional public splurges, funds with hundreds of thousands of shares to unload have only one kind of "customer" to sell to: another equally large fund (or group of funds). So—if you ever thought that there is a group which is constantly plotting against you, if you have contracted the disease of thinking or saying "they" did this or "they" did that—forget it. Most important, realize that your very suspiciousness—the obsession that people are out to "do you in"—is bound to be injurious to you. It will reduce your chances for serenity with your holdings, which in turn is bound to inhibit your money-making potential.

Thus, you should erase any image you might have of the type of characters Eliot Ness* used to handle. The fact is that you don't need Eliot Ness. Instead, you need the kind of thought developed in the last chapter: that of a logical and well-disciplined approach to the stock market. Frankly, that should take care of everything—including the "they" gremlins!

*The fearless FBI ace who, with nine other dedicated men, broke the Mafia's power some forty years ago. These crimebusters became known to the underworld as "The Untouchables," the tales of which became the successful TV series of the same name.

7. Risk Is As Risk Does

Risk, which the dictionary defines as "exposure to the chance of injury or loss," is bound to be a consideration for every investor to ponder—whether he is interested in stocks, real estate, or business. As if that were not enough, the wordbook goes on to state that risk is a "hazard or dangerous chance." So now the fear of God has been implanted in one's mind; and since "risk" and "investments" go together like Jack and Jill, it stands to reason that a very strong element of fear becomes associated with the very thought of investing.

Far be it from me to argue with the dictionary,

but I feel that the definition of risk must be changed —at least when we think in terms of investing our money. Now don't get me wrong. I have no intention of trying to convince you that you should throw caution to the wind and go for broke in your investment approach, giving little or no consideration to the possibilities of loss. Quite the contrary, I have long been a proponent of establishing so-called "risk/reward" ratios for stocks I recommend, and I pride myself on finding equities which are likely to do exceedingly well on the upside without having what I consider to be sizable possibilities on the downside. This philosophy is, to me, one of the real challenges of investing and I don't want you to think for a moment that I am not cognizant of potential for loss.

The point I am coming to, however, is that risks are very relative, and that it is absolutely essential that you understand their relativity. This relativity bit can be explained easily by referring to those billions of dollars in savings accounts on which I commented in chapter 4. I think it is fair to say that almost every one of the millions of savings-account depositors consider their dollars stand little or no risk. At the same time, it is obvious from the opportunities which exist for far higher returns (i.e., Treasury notes and bills, commercial paper, etc.) that these very same savings constitute "idle," or relatively nonproductive, funds. All of which brings us to the query: can idle funds be considered riskless, especially when the cost of living and our society's desire for a higher standard of living are increasing by leaps and bounds?

The answer is obviously no.

The person who placed his money in "riskless" investments such as savings, government bonds, and other idle-type securities at any time over the past twenty-five to thirty years can certainly attest to the fact that he suffered, just as the dictionary states, "injury and loss."

Other things fall into the same pattern. Does Johnny Unitas take a great risk when on fourth down and inches to go, with the defensive backs up close, he throws the "bomb"? Does the tennis player who has an accurate strong serve really take less risk by changing his style and using a patsy, or does he instead find that he either double-faults with the simple serve or that his opponent puts it away? Does a gin-rummy player take less risk through constantly discarding his high face-value cards, or does his opponent learn to anticipate his actions and end up with more melds?

Returning to our subject of investments, does the person who wants to keep up with inflation and who desires improved living conditions take a riskless, totally defensive posture? Not if he wants to accomplish the goals in mind. I wish I had originated the thought the best defense is a strong offense. It certainly is applicable here.

Dr. Maltz observes: "Standing still, failure to act, causes people who are faced with a problem to become nervous, feel 'stymied,' 'trapped,' and can bring on a host of physical symptoms. A step in the wrong direction," he says, "is better than staying 'on the spot' all your life. Once you're moving forward you can correct your course as you go."

In investment terminology, *stop associating risk*

with offensive strategy; if your offense is properly planned, there is far less risk than in a defensive, idle approach.

Let us go back to my Industry Strength Guide of chapter 5. An offense which centers on ownership of strong companies operating within strong industries should carry with it the kind of positive thoughts and forward movement which should in fact minimize risks for you over the years.

This does *not* mean that respectability connotates nonrisk. Some of the most "respectable" companies imaginable—such as General Electric, Du Pont, Union Carbide, and American Telephone—have gone through very risky and unrewarding periods. Actually, an understanding of the guide, plus other factors to be discussed later, would have pointed up the risks which ownership of such companies entailed.

Understanding the Fishbowl

Actually, fear of risk is heightened in the stock market through the mere existence of published daily market prices. As already indicated, stocks exist in a fishbowl. This is an advantage in that it reflects stocks' inherent liquidity, i.e., the ability to purchase or to convert into cash on an immediate basis. But it adds to the emotional adjustments involved, since human greed is stimulated as prices advance and fear and worry enter when prices decline. Naturally it is this latter situation which magnifies risk in the eyes of the stock owner. In contrast, the investor buying a piece of real estate tends to be less nervous. As long as there is full occupancy of an apartment house or an office building, he may not realize that his investment is fluctuating on a daily basis relative to what a buyer might pay for it. He is probably not routinely testing such sales value and fortunately his emotions are not constantly tested due to the fact that no visible daily evaluation is published. I have witnessed absolute dual personalities in hundreds and hundreds of cases over the years—people who were frightened into emotional traumas as a result of posted market prices in a falling stock market, but who worried very little about their real estate even though it, too, was declining in value.

"Stocks Are Only Pieces of Paper"

A contributory factor to the stock worrier can also be the evidence of ownership. I have heard numerous real-estate/stock owners reflect uncertainty over stocks because of the flimsy proof of possession. "Look, all I have to show is a little piece of paper for my stocks; in my real estate, I can see the bricks and mortar" may seem like a weak argument—but it is entirely real to some. Needless to say, the best way to offset this feeling is to recognize what the company representing your stock ownership constitutes. For those with this hangup, an attempt to understand the earning assets of the company will go a long way towards obliterating the piece-of-paper image. Get hold of the company's annual report, which will show you some of these assets, which include buildings, machinery, products, and people. Write the company for a catalogue of products manufactured. Visit either a local plant or a retail outlet which carries the goods which are going to create the sales and earnings. Take a look (see the annual report or Standard & Poor report sheets) at the company's balance sheet and income statement and see just how substantial the outfit really is. All of this will help, both in the prepurchase decision-making process and in an anxiety-free holding period.

To conclude, a proper understanding of risk is essential. You now see that it is a very relative term and that risk tends to increase mainly when you go to the extremes of either idleness or craziness in your investments.

8. On Losing Cold, Hard Dollars

In the last chapter I emphasized that it is essential to understand the relativity of risk in investments. That discussion, however, concerned *indirect* risks—i.e., those which exist in relation to inflation or to what else might be accomplished with the money involved.

Needless to say, these indirect risks are not as compelling or as psychologically disturbing as the direct ones—the actual loss of cold, hard dollars. It is one thing to know that by having had your money in a savings account for years, you have lost relative spending power and missed potential opportunity. It is entirely different to adjust to the fact of a concrete loss, to have invested your money in stocks which today are worth less than you paid for them. Indeed, now we have to talk about real losing.

Any discussion of losing has to start with the frank admission that in some measure it is absolutely inevitable. If you are going to engage in any form of investing you are going to make occasional mistakes and it is important that you prepare yourself emotionally for them.

A starting point, therefore, is to avoid expecting perfect performance from yourself. By realizing that all investors have skeletons in their closets and that we all need erasers on our pencils, you at least eliminate an illusion which could otherwise be very destructive at the time of your first upset. Perfection is an admirable goal but the urge for it can be self-defeating—especially in the area of investments.

The Tendency to Rationalize Losses

The human tendency to rationalize shortcomings, mistakes, and disappointments is of great interest and we could spend many pages exploring it. So far as investing is concerned, too many people have no understanding of themselves when the inevitable failure occurs; and because of this, they react in ways which may produce even more negative results.

The outlet for many involves a rationalizing process which has nothing rational about it. For example, many investors go to the extreme of believing that losses do not exist until they are actually taken.

There are countless stockholders walking the streets today who actually believe that their "paper losses" differ from their "real" losses, and that an unrealized loss is really not a loss at all.

This, of course, is hiding the truth. While one may always hope that a stock will return to its original purchase price, sound investing dictates realistic assessment of conditions on a consistent basis. The wise investor tries at all times to see things as they are and attempts to be flexible enough to roll with the changing punches; for *every investment represents dollars which might be put to work elsewhere.*

The fact is that too many investors go to the greatest extremes to support their original judgment—even after it has been proven incorrect. They duplicate the pattern of the heavy smoker who goes from doctor to doctor until he finds one who tells him that he need not quit because the harm done to his nerves by trying to "kick" the habit will be far more serious than the possibilities of getting heart disease or cancer. Loss-holders will seek comfort through conversations with friends, fellow shareholders, brokers—anyone who will listen and nod affirmatively that the original thinking was correct and that it is the market which is wrong, not them. As a matter of fact, these self-deceivers will accentuate the positive and eliminate the negative from news releases and the statements and statistics released by the company in question. Whereas the astute investor knows that those responsible for corporation financial relations are paid to be positive, the desire on the part of the self-deceiver to obliterate any hint of defeat is so great that he cannot see this obvious truth.

Another part of this rationale is the security-of-dividends argument already discussed in chapter 4. It may well be that the dividend is still being paid and that it is well covered by earnings (it may not be, however), but this is no excuse for saying that the loss is not real and that the investment should not be reassessed.

One other method for easing the *anxieties* of losses is to offset them by taking profits—many times very premature profits. Some people, while recognizing their losses, will never actually take them, but will sell off gain-stocks to erase the trauma of the paper loss. This goes contrary to the theory of cutting losses short and letting profits run, but this does not matter to the individual intent solely on easing his mind. The result, of course, is that his portfolio ends up filled almost exclusively with losers and no winners. Thus, the "jewels" have been sold and the "cats and dogs" remain.

To put all this in terms of Gertrude Stein, a loss is a loss is a loss is a loss. Indeed, whether losses exist on paper or whether they have been taken, they exist and they are real. The important consideration is to view each one objectively and to make investment judgments on them. *The greatest risk of all is to pretend they do not exist and to close your mind to new conditions having a bearing on them and on possible substitutes for them.*

Later on, we will deal with actual losses and with substitute investments. First, let's explore the biggest bugaboo of them all—the *fear* of losses, which inhibits investors so severely.

The Fear of Losing

When I think back over my life and consider the fears which I harbored at various times, I arrive at one obvious conclusion: that the fears were far worse than the realities.

There are two reasons why this is true:

1. Because many of the things feared are never experienced. Thus, if you fear some sort of disaster and it never comes to pass, your fear was certainly greater than the reality—which in this case was nothing at all; and
2. Because the human mind has a tendency to concentrate on whatever input is presented and to exaggerate its tendency.

While the first of these two requires no further explanation, the latter has interesting ramifications. Years ago someone related a story to me which I will never forget, simply because it typifies life, people in general and, most specifically, the normal thinking process of human beings relative to fear and worry. The story concerns a man who is driving across a deserted region of the U.S. and who suddenly has his motor sputter and then stop. Alas, upon checking his gauge he finds that there is no gasoline in the tank. There are no phones around, no trace of anyone—except for an old farmhouse he remembered passing some miles back.

After first deciding that slitting his throat would hardly be productive, the man concludes that the best course of action is to walk back to the farmhouse and secure enough gas from the farmer's private pump to get himself to the next town. So—off he trudges.

As he walks, he thinks about his situation and the problem at hand: getting gas from the farmer. Soon worry creeps in and the man thinks that perhaps the farmer does not possess a pump of his own. Five minutes later another thought strikes him: that the farmer has a pump—but that he is out of fuel at this particular moment. Wouldn't that be a pain in the neck!

A short time later, another fantasy presents itself: maybe the farmer isn't home. Then he thinks: well, maybe he is home—but he's the kind who'll take advantage of a situation like this and charge him twenty or thirty bucks for a gallon of gas. A fine guy, this farmer!

Trudging further, as he begins to feel hot and tired from the hike, the thought arises: suppose the farmer has a pump, the pump is full, he is home—but he just plain won't give me any gasoline. Not even a gallon? No—not even one stinking drop!

Around the corner he walks and here's the farmhouse. The last fifty yards are like eighty miles, as his little old brain is working a mile a minute. Finally on the doorstep, he pounds on the door. And then pounds again.

A second later, the door opens slowly and standing there is a kindly, gray-haired farmer, holding a Bible in one hand. At which time, the man smacks the old farmer right in the face and yells: "You—you miserable rat. You wouldn't even give a measly gallon of gas to a hot, tired, starving guy whose car sits five miles up the road with an empty tank!"

Abnormal?

No, not at all.

For one thing, a brain burdened with too many negatives is not only not as productive as it should be —it may in fact become downright destructive.

Secondly, human beings have a tendency to exaggerate their fears. And anticipatory worry is almost always worse than the potential reality. Franklin Delano Roosevelt summed it up when he said in his First Inaugural Address in March, 1933, when this nation was experiencing a terrible depression, "The only thing we have to fear is fear itself."

On the intriguing subject of money and investments, let me refer for a moment to Mr. Napoleon Hill who, inspired by the multimillionaire Andrew Carnegie, made a study of hundreds of wealthy men. In his famous book, *Think and Grow Rich,* Mr. Hill discusses the six basic human fears: poverty, criticism, ill health, loss of love, old age, and death. Now would you believe Mr. Hill's contention that the most destructive of the six is—the *fear of poverty?*

Now what, you are probably thinking, does poverty have to do with me—or with the subject at hand? Poverty refers to being poor, and those of us considering stock investing are hardly worried about that. Losing a few bucks, yes, but poverty—definitely not! To this I would retort: maybe and maybe not. For one thing, most people do not recognize the basis of their fears. As Hill says, "So subtle and deeply seated is the emotion of fear that one may go through life burdened with it, never recognizing its presence." I would add to this my impressions of the thousands of investors with whom I have had contact in some way: *a basic fear of LOSING, if not of poverty, exists in practically everyone.*

Even assuming that poverty is not our hangup in any way, let us at least hear out the argument and consider the six symptoms of the fear of poverty which *Think and Grow Rich* points up and see whether they are typical of investors.

The Six Symptoms Analyzed

1. *Indifference,* which in this case covers lack of ambition, initiative, imagination, enthusiasm, and/or self-control.

Those billions of dollars in savings and other "no-risk" investments certainly are a measure of this indifference. It has always amazed me to see how many hours people will spend toiling in a variety of ways while at the same time being unwilling to devote themselves to an important subject such as their own financial planning and building.

2. *Indecision,* which Hill describes as "The habit of permitting others to do one's thinking. Staying 'on the fence.' "

Once again, leaving money idle is a result of indecision. Likewise, those horrible annuity vehicles (horrible, that is, unless you plan to live to a very, very ripe old age). Tip-taking is an example of how some people foolishly break out of their indecision. Fearful of making an effort on their own, which might fail, many follow this dangerous route in which the hint of inside information seemingly forces them to act.

3. *Doubt,* which Hill says is: "Generally expressed through alibis and excuses to cover up, explain away, or apologize for one's failures, sometimes expressed in the form of envy of those who are successful, or by criticizing them."

Later on in this book, I will discuss some of the excuses used in stock investing and I will emphasize envy. For the moment, however, just think how many people have blamed the stock market itself for their lack of accomplishment; or the broker; or even the "they" which I talked about in Chapter 6.

4. *Worry,* the greatest manifestation of which is probably nervousness.

This should not require much explanation, other than to say that people tend to be overly nervous when it comes to stocks (more on this later when I tell you how to stay around for the "big winners").

5. *Overcaution* and

6. *Procrastination,* both of which are closely related to the first four and which are explained above.

If you see yourself in any of these six categories there is a strong likelihood that you, too, have some conscious or subconscious fear of poverty (whether it is poverty or simply worry about financial losses, it is obviously restrictive).

By the time you have completed this book you will have sufficient input to negate indifference, indecision, doubt, worry, overcaution, and procrastination. As a matter of fact, we are already on this constructive road—the starting point of which was understanding that the process of approaching the stock market is really logical.

Actually, this is the most important point for those who have the "What if I lose" fear. My advice is to do the bulk of your worrying *before* you have invested rather than after. I would, however, substitute the word "preparation" for "worrying." Do the proper preparation before you have invested and your thinking process throughout ownership of any security will be more positive and simplified.

Limiting Losses Mechanically

On this same subject, people frequently ask about the use of stop-loss orders in the market. (Stop-loss allows you to limit your loss by having your stock automatically sold after it has declined by a fixed amount of your choice; thus, if you wish to limit your loss on Xerox to 10 percent of today's purchase at eighty dollars per share, you set a stop-loss sell order with your broker at seventy-two dollars, and if Xerox falls to that figure your stock is automatically sold at that time).

I consider the stop-loss one of the worst manifestations of a stock-market inferiority complex. If you feel so insecure about buying Xerox that you have to limit yourself to 10 percent on the downside, you really should not buy it. Maybe the dollars you are investing are too crucial, in which case you shouldn't be investing at all (more on this in chapter 14). Certainly there is something that is worrying you into foolish behavior, for the chances are excellent that you will be sold out in any temporary dip in the market or in a general decline—and most times this will happen when you should be buying the very stock you are selling. What is more, this approach tends to make you more active than you should be; through the device of a stop-loss, you make yourself into a flitting buyer and seller of stocks.

This is not to say that an investor should close his eyes to loss and stubbornly adhere to the thinking which made him buy the stock in the first place. There are many occasions when a 10 percent loss saves you from something much larger. But your reason for selling should not hinge solely on an arbitrary percentage figure. Just as there are times when you should sell with a large gain—and pay the taxes, and there are times when you should sell for a 5 percent loss even a few short weeks after purchase, your judgment of the matter should go beyond merely a predetermined percentage figure.

In a way, the stop-loss is like Gene Tunney's battles with Jack Dempsey. When you concentrate too heavily on your opponent's right hand, which might finish you, you neglect your own attack—something which Tunney discovered only after almost losing his first fight to the Manassa Mauler. Subsequent to this, however, he changed his thinking and instead of concentrating on the negative side of the situation, i.e., Dempsey's killing punch, he constructed a positive plan of his own—which then brought him the championship. In stock-market jargon, he stopped worrying about limiting his losses and concentrated on proper strategy and selection.

Limiting Loss Anxieties

While an offensive strategy is ideal, this does not mean that there is no room for a defense against either actual losses or against the anxieties which the fear of loss creates.

I start out with the premise that *a person should never take a chance which will endanger his prospects for living exactly the way he wants to live.* Thus, if you can define reasonable wants—omitting pie-in-the-sky desires such as owning castles and villas all over the world—and you have already achieved these wants, you now have a strong responsibility to preserve your achievement—both for yourself and those dependent on you. This is not to say that at such a juncture equities should be shifted to fixed-income securities. But it does mean that both a mathematical and a psychological effort should be made to retain the happy status you have achieved.

Mathematically, you can determine just how many dollars you can lose without having your mode of living altered—and then set about to structure your portfolio so that this loss is highly unlikely (perhaps by setting aside sufficient dollars in riskless, higher-yielding securities such as Treasury bills or by shifting from very speculative common stocks to others which will at least pay their way if the market collapses). The person who does not do this must frankly admit that greed has overruled good judgment.

One good test of what you can afford to lose is to pretend that you have already sustained a loss. Pick a figure, assume your assets have declined by that amount, and see how both the numbers *and* your emotions are affected. If the figures are frightening then the chance is not worth taking.

These are approaches which too few people followed over the past few years in the stock market. Many people had it made as a result of 1968's bull market, but many forgot that trees do not grow to the sky and just kept taking chances. That they risked both economic and emotional serenity was obvious from the panic which resulted from the collapse of the 1970 market. While the dollar drain was bad, just as bad was the emotional havoc the dollar drain created.

Whereas the foolishness of risking status may not need further amplification, its seriousness forces me to emphasize the point. Hoping that you will not consider me morose, let me go to an extreme and relate this to the unpleasant subject of suicide.

All of us have memories of certain unfortunate people who have lost large sums of money; and all of us have at least heard about persons who have taken their lives for what has been explained as financial reasons. The explanations for such a drastic act by a human being are extremely complicated and go way beyond what might appear to be the ostensible motive for the act. Still, studies have shown that suicide occurs far more often at the top of the economic ladder than at the bottom. Indeed, a renowned textbook, *Clues to Suicide,** presents data proving "that

*Edwin S. Shneidman and Norman L. Farberow, *Clues to Suicide* (New York: McGraw-Hill, 1957).

susceptibility to suicide rises with status position." And in another book dealing with *Suicide in London** the author found that the areas with the highest suicide rates in that city "were those with the highest proportion of middle-class, moderately well-to-do inhabitants."

I tell you this not to alarm you, but to make you fully aware that anyone playing with the happiness and serenity his earnings have brought him should be fully cognizant of the risks involved.

Two Other Loss Limiters: Do Nothing and Do Everything

At this point "Nothing ventured, nothing lost" should be understood as no solution to the problem of making money. The procrastinator expresses his doubts and worries through a do-nothing indifference and indecision which, of course, will get him exactly what he bargains for. In a way, procrastination is like our computer GIGO example: put nothing in, get nothing out!

Many people with the same fears react in a totally opposite manner by overdiversifying, or doing everything. Down deep the over-diversifier is saying, "I haven't the time, the inclination, or the knowledge to make the best decisions on a limited number of holdings; but if I buy enough stocks I am bound to hit some good ones." While some diversification is sound practice and does reduce the extremes of anx-

*Peter Sainsbury, *Suicide in London* (New York: Basic Books, 1955).

iety, buying a host of securities will lead to no better than mediocre performance. Supervision is difficult, the mechanics are arduous, and the good performers will be cancelled out by the poor ones. It's a case of chicken and egg: whether laziness leads to overdiversification or whether overdiversification leads to laziness, the method is weak. Of the thousands of portfolios I have seen over the years I cannot remember one with a do-everything approach which accomplished much for its owner.

On Exaggerating Losses

Still on the subject of losses, the way in which people exaggerate the monetary declines which they experience is amazing—and sad. I have seen investors with many, many dollars—even millions—become emotionally distraught over the loss of a few thousand; and I have seen people with assets in the thousands get very uptight over the loss of a few hundred.

The fact is that people tend to lose their perspective when it comes to dollars. Take the case of Mr. Down-in-the-dumps, who had a portfolio of stocks worth about $30,000. On his list he held one security which was down in value around $1,000 from its original cost. Down-in-the-dumps would not sell the stock and yet he proceeded to pester and berate his broker until the latter asked me to step in and calm the poor fellow down.

The next day Mr. D appeared in my office and spent the first five minutes in a monologue about this particular thorn in his side. The fact that the $1,000 loss amounted to just 3 percent of his total holdings and that the rest of his portfolio was in fine shape was of no consequence to him. It was the $1,000 "bath" which was disturbing him. After ten minutes it finally struck me what Down-in-the-dumps' problem was. *He was adding negative opinion to the facts.* It was not the $1,000 at all that was bugging him. Rather he had supplied in his mind some inputs which were disgracing him—i.e., that the stupidity involved in the original purchase decision was so great that it branded him as some sort of inferior creature. Thus, the disgrace, stupidity, and inferiority magnified beyond reason the amount of the lost dollars. Mr. Down-in-the-dumps had carried spilled-milk-itis so far he was destroying himself.

Thus, *you should not let self-esteem and pride become so tied to your investing that a loss has a traumatic effect on your day-to-day living and happiness.*

Throwing in the Towel

The one thing we know for certain about the stock market is—that it will fluctuate. Up and down it goes, in response to business prospects, world happenings, inflation, politics, and a host of other factors. Most important, and this constitutes the thesis of this book, is the market's sensitivity to human emotions and psychology. Herein lies the most undeveloped portion of the subject, the understanding of which can do wonders for you.

The psychological framework of most investors makes them:

1. React in different, and sometimes diametrically opposed, ways to a similar set of circumstances at any given time; and this
2. Leads to opposite extremes in their attitude towards individual stocks and the market as a whole.

In a way, both of these statements say the same thing—that often there is little rationale for market action other than the mood of the moment. Prime examples of this are the sharp drops which occurred in stocks at the time of the Eisenhower heart attack in 1955 and the Kennedy assassination in 1963. In both cases the Dow-Jones Industrial Average plummeted over thirty points, and many individual issues lost between 15 and 25 percent of their value. Yes, 15 to 25 percent in one day! Significant and unfortunate as the events responsible were, it is more than just hindsight which tells me that such changes are hardly ever deserved. And yet emotions and panic at the moment were such as to create them.

There are countless experiences that illustrate how investors react in different ways to a given set of circumstances. Take something as confusing as legal action against a large and attractive company like Bristol-Myers. Proposed settlement of a large price-fixing suit on penicillin against Bristol-Myers, American Cyanimid, and Charles Pfizer had little bearing on the former's common-stock action when the market's general mood was optimistic in 1968. Yet in early 1970, when stockholders were nervous generally, announcement of a relatively small suit involving a maximum of $13 million caused Bristol-Myers' common to drop almost six points in one day; these six points, when multiplied by each of the company's 50 million shares outstanding, amounted to a $300 million downward evaluation. Thus, a large lawsuit during a good market had no effect on the stock and a small one at the time of a different mood created a serious market decline.

Mr. Leo Model, the sage leader of the investment firm of Model, Roland & Co. of New York, once pointedly summarized this phenomenon. According to Model, the *facts* relating to securities, the fundamentals of earnings and dividends and book value, are but a portion of the mechanics leading to the end result. He rephrases and simplifies the message of this book—and the crux of this chapter—by stating that high prices are usually no more than *Facts plus Hope;* and that low prices are often the very same *Facts,* this time *plus Fear.*

Lastly, and most important, individuals (in large numbers) are *prone to throw in the towel for reasons other than their opinion of a stock at any given time.* It goes without saying that you should give up—and give up fast—on a stock in which you have altered your basic opinion. This is different from a decision to give up *just to erase a mistake from your thinking* —something which happens all the time at the very end of a bear market (which is, of course, just when a person should be buying, not selling).

I have heard people say, over and over, that they want to sell XYZ "because I don't want to worry about it any more." Indeed, stockholders at near the conclusion of down markets in 1958, 1962, 1966 and

1970 simply threw in stocks, without regard for price or prospects, in order to erase the unpleasant memory associated with a sharp drop in market price.

Needless to say, it is essential for you to understand and recognize this "throw in the towel—erase the memory" tendency. It will help you in dealing with difficult markets, it will possibly encourage you to fight the crowd when you witness others following such a rationale, and it will make you a more sophisticated investor in that you will recognize and understand the mass psychology which dictates stock prices.

The Dangers of Labels and How to Handle Blame for Losses

Human beings tend to think in generalities. In the process they utilize "labels" which can inhibit their open-mindedness in the future. E.g., the Italians are one thing, the Germans another. Doctors are one way, attorneys some other. Artists are this, and athletes are that. And, of course, the chemicals are ______ and the drugs are ______. And Avon is this and General Motors that.

We are all entitled to expressions which shorten our method of description, but these labels can be dangerous—especially when things are not going as we would like, when we are seeking a scapegoat, when we need to find an outlet for our displeasure.

Politicians and athletes certainly understand this labeling tendency. Some voters and some fans possess compassion for unpleasantries, but most people are quick to blame others for anything short of perfection. Politicians are lauded one minute and damned the next. Athletes find their supporters at one game are the "boo-birds" of the next. In short, the human need to vent displeasure is generally so great that it obliterates successful efforts of the past, leading to most ungentlemanly behavior and some potentially destructive labeling.

We already discussed how certain investors blame the market for their own naïveté or poor judgment. In addition, many place such unattractive labels on securities which have treated them poorly that objectivity in the future is practically impossible. "The chemicals are 'dogs' " or "G.E. is a lousy stock" will only restrict the kind of liberal judgment which should constitute the base of proper investment thinking.

This book provides you with an approach which will help to separate the real "dogs" from those which are being labeled that due to disappointment or misfortune. (Remember that some stocks do poorly because the company has not performed, while others are the product of nothing but investor over-enthusiasm—which is usually the investor's fault, not the company's.)

You can become a far more efficient investor simply by recognizing the blaming processes of others; and, equally important, by understanding the elation response which comes from winning. The language of investing goes through a total transformation as stocks or the general market swing from gain to loss and back again. For example, when profits of a stainless steel producer are rising rapidly investors might label it a glamorous "specialty metals" company. A year later, when earnings are dropping, the same entity becomes a "crummy steel." Forest-products stocks might be termed "great natural resource" outfits when the building/paper cycle is favorable; but the same situations suddenly become "unattractive commodity" investments when conditions worsen. Under favorable conditions food companies "fill the need to feed the world"—but during normal times "the field is mundane."

The lesson, therefore, goes way beyond converting you from a possible bad loser to a good loser. The famous comedian Joe E. Lewis used to kid: "Show me a good loser and I'll show you . . . A LOSER!" There is a happy medium between being such a bad loser that it is destructive and being so oblivious to losses that you lack the ambition to school yourself to better performance.

Developing a proper offense demands objectivity. Part of this entails understanding that this week's loser is probably going to be labeled "a bum," but that the same stock may be next year's hero. The solution lies in an objective assessment of fundamentals and an understanding of how securities attain labels according to recent fortunes or misfortunes. This understanding helps you keep your head during general markets which have been blown out of proportion with either pessimism or optimism. And it develops the strength needed to buck a trend resulting from others' blaming and ballooning individual stocks. An astute investor recognizes the dangers of scapegoats and broad generalities; he sees through the dangerous labels which emanate from them; and he conditions himself to take advantage of the bargains and over-evaluations which result from them.

Conclusions

Obviously some losses are inevitable. It sounds Pollyanna-ish to suggest that we can learn from such mistakes, but of course we can. Equally important—and part of this learning process—is the ability to relax with our investments. Whereas the gunslinger days of 1968 bred nervousness into the marrow of many stock buyers—and whereas the price which was paid for the overexuberance of these days led to a natural nervousness through part of 1969 and 1970—the most successful money managers I know have learned how to relax with well-chosen securities. This will be discussed in greater detail in chapter 18, but for the time being your understanding of losses, the natural human reactions to them, and how to deal with them should go a long way towards making you a better-adjusted investor.

A Loss Questionnaire for Investors

Both as an aid to opening you up to yourself and as a discipline, I have prepared a short "Loss Questionnaire" which I urge you to complete right now. Please answer the following four queries:

1. *a.* I am trying to prove something about myself and my own abilities when I invest;
   b. I am investing because it is an interesting "game";
   c. I am investing so as to achieve a decent rate of return on my money over the years.
2. *a.* I believe losses do not exist until the underlying security is actually sold;
   b. I always sell my loss securities very early;
   c. I assess my losers just as I assess my winners —on the basis of an objective appraisal of conditions.
3. *a.* I assess my investment results on the basis of what Schedule D on my income-tax form shows;
   b. I never count losses or gains until they are "taken";
   c. I consider my losses as a whole against my gains as a whole in determining investment results.
4. *a.* I find it easier to reach a decision if I have a profit;
   b. I find it easier to reach a decision if I have a loss;
   c. I make my decision based on something other than gain or loss position.

Giving yourself one point for *a* and *b* answers, and two points for *c* answers, anything less than five or six points means you had best reread this chapter. Ideally, you should have answered *c* on at least the final three questions; if you did not, go back to them and figure out why *c* should be your response.

9. Who Is Looking Over Your Shoulder? Or "Yes, Dear" Or On Establishing Correct "Investual Relations"

While on the subject of worry and the fear of loss, we should explore other factors which might contribute to such pressures. The next few chapters, all very short, will do just this.

The first which comes to mind is indeed a very delicate subject in that it touches on family relationships, especially that between husband and wife.

Now I know that all of you who *are* married are enjoying the ultimate in marital bliss—and far be it from me to disturb this utopian situation. I am afraid, however, that I will have to enter your bedroom for just a moment and invade your private lives.

Relax!

I have not discovered any link between stock-market success and sexual relations; and I have no intention of conducting a new Kinsey Report. What I am interested in knowing has to do with what I term "Investual" Relations—which involves the kind of communication between two married people having to do with their investments. (How Victorian of me—it can relate to unmarrieds, too.)

Believe it or not, "Investual Relations" may become almost as touchy as sexual relations in that the former broaches the delicate subject of Man or Mouse.*

What I am laboring to say is that a person can (and will) be severely restricted in his stock-market behavior if someone is breathing heavily down his neck and looking over his shoulder too closely.†

Seriously, over-the-shoulder looking can make a Caspar Milquetoast out of a John Wayne. Constant sniping and too-close scrutiny of one's investments can serve to make a mousy investor out of anyone.

Before the League of Women Voters, the Daughters of the American Revolution, the women's liberation movement, and every other female organization in the country swoops down on me, let me

*The fact that the former (Investual Relations) is capitalized and the latter (sexual relations) is in lower case in no way indicates the author's lack of respect for the latter, nor does it indicate the author's opinion that the former will replace the latter in any way, nor does it preclude anyone—including the author—from engaging in both, either at the same time or separately.

†See, we're getting there already. We started at the neck and already we're down to the shoulder. Who knows—maybe Investual Relations and sexual relations are one and the same. Advice: You had better read on.

make it clear that women can be excellent investors and in some cases their judgment is far superior to that of men. So if your family is one in which mama does the investing, then papa—you just stay wherever you are and quit second-guessing the "old lady."

As a general rule, I think it is safe to say that, in the vast majority of cases, the one with pants generally handles the investing. And from what I have observed over the years, that is just as well. Women, God love them, do tend to be more emotional than men—and of course they suffer from the fact that they are not engaged in day-to-day business, which after all is the backbone of the market itself. Furthermore, women do not spend as much time in their lives involved in winning and losing ventures (i.e., gambling). And talk about Fear of Poverty—well, that's much more developed in the female than the male (and for good reason—since women are not usually the breadwinners, to begin with).

Of course, these shortcomings are hardly female monopolies. We can all strengthen our understanding of business (particularly as it relates to stock investing), of winning and losing, and of the many emotional barriers which must be overcome in order to succeed. All these roadblocks are discussed in this book and solutions for both male and female are included.

Back to Second-Guessing

Back to the subject of communications, you must realize that *second-guessing creates a tension and a nervousness which is highly injurious to the person trying to perform.* This is true whether the second-guessing be between client and broker or between client and client's spouse. Far be it from me to psychoanalyze the second-guesser, but he places the "guessee" in the position of being damned if he does and damned if he does not. As in any pursuit, confidence is a strong factor in investing, and the second-guesser breaks this down substantially.

I have seen this phenomenon exist in a vast number of instances. With my own clients I can compare how I have done for those who have given me carte blanche versus those who may have assented to this arrangement but who then could not resist the urge to call in and question why certain steps were being taken; these inquiries invariably come when stock prices are dropping generally or when success is coming quickly. These are just the times when the captain of the ship needs to direct his own course with a minimum of outside emotional inputs. The performance of those accounts which have relaxed with my direction is far superior to those that have interfered.

An excellent example of the second-guessing syndrome is offered by the performance of certain mutual funds which have divided their portfolios among a number of individual money managers, *but where top management has not really allowed proper discretion for the new managers.* I know of one billion-dollar outfit which did this, but where the former manager kept putting in his two cents worth, consequently making the new captain feel he was being constantly second-guessed. In taking on the portfolio, the man admitted privately to me that he had "inherited a leper colony" of stocks in which he had little detailed knowledge or personal conviction. Yet he had to justify to his former boss the sale of many stocks which had been the latter's personal choices.

The result was a disaster for the fund. The new money manager felt the breath of his superior down his neck and he was fearful of alienating him—when, in fact, he should have cleaned house and kept only those securities in which he had total confidence. One of the good rules of strong money management is that you should only hold those stocks which you would buy today—which is just the opposite of what happened in this situation. As indicated, the outcome was most unfortunate as the fund dropped significantly in value in 1969 and 1970 and was near the bottom of the industry's Hit Parade during this period.

Achieving the Happy Medium

This is not to say that there is no room for discussion among counterparts to a common goal. Communication and understanding are essential elements in any program, investments included. But self-esteem and domestic relations should not be confused with investment results. Husband and wife should discuss goals and achievements together, just as people in business should. It is important, however, to distinguish between working together in one area and defining responsibility. To put it more bluntly, the person designated to be the boss of investments should really be the boss. The combination of an understanding of goals with a clear definition of who is boss constitutes successful Investual Relations. And this approach is pertinent right through to the management of institutional dollars. As you might expect, a rational approach to the market on the part of the boss will do wonders to create confidence on behalf of the party of the second part. Which is just where our Psycho-Cybernetic inputs come in: assimilation of these inputs will provide you with that very rational approach to making money in the stock market; this in turn will clear the path for Investual Relations at its best.

10. The House With The Golden Windows

Once upon a time there was a family which lived in a nice house—yes, a very nice house. Along with the house they possessed enough assets to enjoy the amenities of life; with this and their personal compatabilities, they should have been a most happy family. Which, unfortunately, they were not.

The reason for their miserable existence stemmed from just one source—which was a little old house which was located a mile or so away from theirs.

Each day when the family gathered around five

or six o'clock—after papa had returned home from work, mama had finished her bridge game, and Junior had ambled home from school—they would settle in their front room and gaze across at the aforementioned abode. The attraction of this house was simply that it possessed *golden windows.* Yes—bright, beautiful golden windows.

"Why can't *we* have golden windows?" inquired Junior.

"Why can't *we* have such beauty, instead of our old, uninteresting glass?" bleated mama.

"Look at that house," lamented papa. "Here I spent all the money on this place and I never even thought about the windows. I should have thought about getting something unusual—like those golden jobs."

Each night, the three of them found different ways to describe their plight in not having golden windows. Invariably the subject lasted right through dinner—and even beyond. And they became very unhappy because of that little shack with the exciting golden glass.

This went on for months. Until late one afternoon when mama, although obsessed with those windows, suddenly remembered that she needed some goodies for dinner. With all the tact of a dissatisfied person, she daintily said to papa, "Get your big fanny off the sofa and go to the store for me," shoving a scribbled shopping list into his hand.

So papa pulled himself away from the magnet of the golden-windowed house, dragged himself into the car, and sped off to the supermarket. As he drove, his thoughts went back to the subject of windows and he kept repeating to himself, "Gee, I wish we had golden windows."

After traveling twelve or fourteen blocks, he decided to stop the car and look back to see his own house and to compare it with the "golden one." And that he did.

You know, of course, what he saw: that he, too, had golden windows! That what they had been coveting all these months had been no more than the sunset reflected off the windows of the other establishment. And that, of course, the jealousy and the grudging had really been for naught—to say nothing of it having been totally destructive.

What we are talking about is no more than envy —a little four-letter word which can be as destructive as almost any other term you can think of.

Let me make it clear that this book is not intended to take the form of a sermon. I know very well that I don't have to lecture you on the evils of envy. The reason I bring it up, naturally, relates to its ruinous effects on so many investors. The monetary successes of others, plus a tendency on the part of many towards greed, plus an inherent worry about security on the part of so many all point to a "Why can't I have golden windows?" thought process.

To rid ourselves of this tendency, we need only realize a few important points. The first has to do with the monetary successes of others. Some people around you will actually be succeeding, and we simply want to live our own lives and not concern ourselves with them (better said, learn to be happy for them). Probably the worst influence we get from others emanates from the blabbermouth who is constantly bragging about his accomplishments. If this is your problem, just remember that inveterate horse players have the same hangup; you always hear about the ten to one shot which came from last to first in the most beautiful stretch run ever seen—but you seldom hear about the final results of their "study," which in 999 cases of 1,000 means *losing* money.

What then about the problem of eliminating envy that results from basic feelings of (financial) insecurity? Said another way, some people get envious of others' security, not realizing that this security can be theirs, too. Certainly the organized approach which we have presented is one way to know that security can be ours. Another input has to do with the amazing results which consistent savings can bring for you over a period of time. Do you realize, for example, that a forty-year-old person need only put away $67.50 per month in order to end up with $50,000 when he reaches sixty-five—assuming an average 8 percent rate of return on these dollars along the way? And if one can achieve 10 or 15 percent on his money, which, as you will read later, I consider a reasonable expectation, then you will either:

a. realize a much larger sum than $50,000; or
b. require fewer years to reach the goal; or
c. need smaller periodic saving.

Naturally, if you can stash away a few hundred a month, the potential is most exciting.

Thus, for those who experience envy because in essence there is a basic insecurity about finances in the future—take heart! Your windows are more golden than you think; or at least they can be golden.

11. On Kicking Oneself In The Pants

One constant worldwide pastime is the habit of kicking oneself in the pants. Indeed, "Why did I do this?" and "Why didn't I do that?" and "If only I had done this" and "If only I hadn't done that" steal literally millions of hours each year from time which should be put to better use.

Such pants-kicking is evident in everything from business to marriage to gambling to sports to world military involvements—and the stock market is no exception. As a matter of fact, the market constitutes a most fertile ground for the kind of weeds which this thinking produces in the garden of human behavior.

Consider, for example, the multitude of choices available to anyone contemplating investment. The New York Stock Exchange alone presents some 1,400 choices, ranging alphabetically all the way from Abacus Fund to Zurn Industries; and there are many more thousands of companies available through the other stock exchanges and the over-the-counter markets. You can place your dollars in everything from Syntex—whose major product is intended to prevent the birth of babies—to Gerber's and Johnson & Johnson—who aim to feed, bathe, and care for the little rascals who escape the pill.

Within this complex, stock brokers generally give their clients some choice of securities, while the customers themselves are constantly striving to come up with their own beauties. Thus, there is an endless number of possibilities; and since the more possibilities there are, the more potential pants-kicking there is, you can understand the conflicts which the active investor faces.

In addition, the fishbowl existence of the stock market creates further problems. They say that what you don't know will not hurt you, but even a glance at the financial section of the newspaper in itself opens the gates of temptation. Merely following one's investments opens vistas of other securities; for example, clients bring stocks to my attention simply because they have noted the market action of something nearby in the price lists. The guy who owns Polaroid notices that Planning Research is plummeting, but he also sees that Plough is rising and that Potlatch Forests and Procter & Gamble are booming.

All of them are potential pants-kickers, which is just another way of saying that stock investors must learn to understand how and why this pattern evolves, what effect it is liable to have on you, and, most important, *what to do about it.*

What we are really talking about here is self-deprecation, which is the act of expressing disapproval of ourselves and which tends to belittle that great guy we choose to be. From an amateur psychiatric view, this self-deprecation might well stem from the basic feelings of inferiority most of us harbor and from the fact that we all have buried memories of past problems and failures which we would just as soon keep buried. This is not to say that the storage of errors is dangerous; quite the contrary, such recognition is the foundation of learning and of day-to-day actions (hopefully the negative input comes out when we need it and prevents us from repeating the error). The important thing is to have such negative memories in their proper place—which means that they are to be tucked away in a corner. To use a worn-out adage, "Let sleeping dogs lie."

So far as our subject of successful investing is concerned, a person must realize that constant pants-kicking constitutes an effort to remember and even magnify (rather than forget) this kind of negative input. As such, it constitutes the opposite of a Psycho-Cybernetic approach. Furthermore, concentrating on the negative leads to the kind of anticipatory worry discussed in chapter 8. When this pattern exists, an investor will probably develop a "Was I a damned fool" reaction each time a stock is bought or sold—something which will create the very tensions which we wish to avoid in our market commitments.

Closely related to this is the Monday morning quarterback, who instead of learning from mistakes and immediately thinking how his knowledge will aid him in his next effort, simply dwells on the water which is now miles beyond the dam.

The Psycho-Cybernetic solution to this is to store the necessary data and to rely on the kind of positive inputs which should constitute a greater and greater part of our personalities. As the English novelist, George Eliot, stated: "It's but little good you'll do, watering last year's crops." Indeed, there are new stock crops available at any given moment and your concentration on these, with the kind of investment philosophy being presented here, will bring up real vegetation in time.

Some Dangerous Kidding on the Square

Apropos self-deprecation, I have noticed a group of investors who are more subtle in their berating but who are definitely restricting their own performance without knowing it. I refer to a group of great kidders who utilize certain verbal expressions which in themselves might be partly responsible for their disappointing stock-market experiences.

Typical phraseology of these kidders might be: "Do *you* own any Bristol-Myers? If so, it's time to unload. *I* just bought some today." or "Here's some foolproof advice. If you want to make a killing, buy all you can of Polaroid. I just sold mine."

These fellows make a vain attempt at being the Jack Bennys of the investment world—all the time making themselves the brunt of their quips. And all the time saying that when they sell, it's time to buy —and vice versa. And that they always seem to buy at the top and sell at the bottom.

Pretty funny, eh? Absolutely hysterical! The only trouble is that no one is laughing, least of all themselves. For what they are really saying is: "The 'kiss of death.' That's me!"

Some books provide you with ABCs for organized learning. Here are "5 Cs" for those interested in common stocks:

Confine Comedy Concerning Common stocks to the Constructive.

If you don't follow this advice you will probably end up like the golfer with the banana-ball slice who constantly jokes that someday his drive is going to curve right back and smack him in the face. As he thinks he is a slicer, he will indeed continue to be one!

Later on, we will establish some self-talk which is a good deal more productive than either the stock-market kidder or the slicing duffer. For the moment, however, simply realize that the negative kidding, like self-deprecation, is self-defeating and that it should be avoided.

12. Luck Be A Lady

Among the all-time great scenes from musical comedy has to be the one from *Guys and Dolls* when on-the-outs Sky Masterson prepares himself for his crucial venture to the Biltmore Garage to participate in the "oldest established, permanent floating crap game in New York." Sky sings what is now a classic, "Luck Be a Lady."

Certainly I have no intention of comparing stock investing with a crap game, although there are plenty of people who approach the market just this way. Furthermore, the organized methodology I have been offering makes no mention of luck or fate.

Still, as you will now see, an understanding of luck and an attitude towards it can have a strong bearing on you as an investor.

To clear the air, let's face up to the fact that luck *does* play a significant role in investing. To begin with, there are obviously thousands of securities available for purchase in the marketplace, many of which are fairly similar; since you cannot afford to buy them all—and since you should only own a few dozen at the most anyway—you are bound to make decisions which exclude both big losers and big winners which you could well have purchased.

In addition, since it is impossible to judge day-to-day fluctuations which occur in the market, luck has a lot to do with what price you pay for a stock or what you sell it for.

And, yes, sometimes luck even overrules what appears to be excellent judgment. Anyone who is truly honest with himself will attest to the fact that oftentimes when he is right, it is really for the *wrong* reason. And many times when you are proven wrong, this is for the wrong reason, too.

Right or wrong, if you observe the market long enough you should develop a deep sense of humility. Stock investing is an *in*exact science, if it is a science at all. This hardly detracts, however, from the wisdom of making a study of it and from building disciplines which can hike your batting average considerably over the years.

Now we have already discussed at length how people blame their inadequacies and/or specific mistakes on outside influences—the most important of which are usually lumped into the one term *bad luck*. As a matter of fact, you could probably fill New York City—and maybe Chicago and Los Angeles, too —with those who either consciously or subconsciously believe that some part of their life is hexed by tough luck. And when it comes to stock ownership, there are countless numbers who likewise believe that such a hex exists.

This really should *not* be the case. Napoleon Hill contends that no one is doomed to bad luck in making money. He says, "There are millions of people who believe themselves 'doomed' to poverty and failure, because of some strange force over which they believe they have no control." Most important, he continues, "They are the creators of their own misfortunes, because of this negative belief, which is picked up by the subconscious mind, and translated into its physical equivalent."

Obviously, Hill's contention is an extreme view and one that perhaps applies to pursuits less abstract and complex than investing in the stock market. This is not to imply that you cannot make your breaks in the latter. You can! But just as Psycho-Cybernetics must be specially adapted so as to apply to correct stock investing procedure, one's view of luck too must be somewhat altered—which we will discuss in a moment.

As with any goal, negativism hampers achievement—so let's explore the derivation of worry which so many seem to possess about hard luck.

No doubt some people pick up the bad luck image from something in their early youth. Maybe they lost playing marbles and associated this defeat with luck rather than lesser skill. Or perhaps they blew the few pennies of change from mother's grocery shopping by pitching coins against the wall (oh, the fear of coming home without those coppers). Or a variety of tiny incidents might have implanted in their minds the idea that they were prone to defeat or to bad luck.

Or perhaps (and I would suggest, very probably) what a large number of individuals have called bad luck is merely a statistical miscalculation. For example, the person who sits in an audience waiting for five tickets to be drawn from a bowl of thousands may consider himself unlucky not to hear his name, whereas he is not unlucky at all—it is just that the odds against his winning are tremendous to begin with. The same thing can be said for any professional gambling, wherein the "house" has the percentages working for it right from the start.

Or maybe, hard as it is to believe, the person cursing ill fortune has simply pitted himself against someone who is more proficient than he at the venture in question. I know people who have been losing money consistently to friends for thirty or forty years and who cannot face up to the fact that their bad luck is no more than their pal's superior ability in the game. (Incidentally, the smart player encourages this self-pity and rationale by sympathizing with his opponent's "tough breaks.")

Lastly, there are probably many individuals who start a project fearing misfortune merely because they want to ready themselves for any failure before it actually occurs. Put another way, they hesitate to anticipate *good* fortune because if it then escapes them, they face bitter disappointment—something which frightens them excessively (here we have another example of how anticipatory worry is destructive).

Whatever the reason, the fact is that luck is many, many times no more than placing yourself in the right spot at the right time, and with the *right attitude.* And bad luck is just the opposite!

Thus, it is essential to understand how an anticipation of bad luck will create such tensions that the misfortunes will become inevitable; just as Mr. Hill said, those who believe themselves doomed to bad luck will in turn have exactly what they are "wishing" on themselves.

Obviously, when tensions vanish and one feels luck is with him, then he will tend to perform well. The best gamblers will tell you that there are times when you "feel" things are going right and that this attitude in itself leads to better play and increased success. The same thing goes for athletics of all sorts. The best athletes possess confidence in themselves and approach their performances with that winning feeling. The powerful term "momentum," which individuals and teams gather (or lose), is a sweeping mental attitude which is merely an extension of the expectation of good luck (or bad luck) in the battle at hand. More important, the stock market becomes a great vehicle for those who condition their luck by seeing that they are generally in the right stocks in the right industries—and then maximize their performance through having the correct attitude about good fortune. Stated differently, if your stock-market "machinery" is success-oriented, your results will show it.

Just in case you have some of the hurdles to overcome which were mentioned on pages 115–17, think about your prospects this way. The statistics are with you, not against you, in the stock market for the following reasons:

1. The law of supply and demand is decidedly favorable to high-quality companies which are still growing. Both individuals and institutions prefer buying and/or holding these securities—as opposed to selling them.

2. Pension-fund and other so-called institutional money is growing by leaps and bounds and is pretty much forced to look positively on fine stocks with the characteristics just described.

3. Bull (upward) markets have dominated the picture over the long range; they have lasted far longer than bear (down) markets.

4. So long as the U.S. economy has an upward tendency, the market itself should have the same basic tendency.

These points are not meant as a chamber of commerce pitch for buying equities nor do they imply that markets are anything resembling a one-way street. As already mentioned, some losses are inevitable—but you would not be wise to associate these with the inevitability of bad luck on your part.

The solution revolves around your preparation and approach. Instead of operating blindly, you should know something about what you are buying and you should know why you have bought it (more on this later); you should remain current on overall industry and company developments; and you should have some clear idea of the rate of return you hope for on your dollars, as well as on the risks being faced. In broad terms, you should be following a logical, well-disciplined, and positive approach to stock investing. Once this is true, I think you will find, as Sky Masterson did, that Lady Luck can be with you. Maybe it will escape you tonight or tomorrow, but it should accompany you generally over the years.

13. The Folly Of Gambling In The Stock Market

It will come as no news to you that investors follow a multitude of approaches in their stock-market efforts. Some buy stocks and never look at them again, stubbornly assuming either that they are correct in their selection and that, by Jove, time will prove this; or that stock certificates are like family heirlooms and are never to be disturbed. Some invest in an organized manner such as that prescribed in this book. Some take part simply "for the hell of it," looking at the market purely as a game. Some go for broke and buy nothing but the most speculative stocks imaginable. Some attempt to trade on a short-term basis, emphasizing day-to-day, week-to-week, or month-to-month action for everything they purchase.

My design here is to concentrate on the last three groups mentioned which, under analysis, are really throwing the dice in their approach to stock investing. We are, then, about to concentrate on the so-called traders and gunslingers in the stock market. And while you may not qualify for either category, I urge you to read on as the points covered apply to all types of investors.

Easy Money

A starting point for discussion is something which relates to practically everyone—the desire for easy money. I suppose it is innate to seek *easy anything;* the important adjustment, and a sign of mature thinking, is to recognize that easy paths are not feasible for everything. Many substantial goals require hard work, and *the person who continually follows the easiest road is the one who generally will accomplish the least.* Relating this to investing, the individual who takes the simplest path—either through merely placing his money in the bank or through investing without effort or forethought—is the one who will end up with the fewest chips at the end.

Typical of the easy-money seeker is the tiptaker, the person who centers his investment life around tips from a variety of sources. It is interesting —though sad—to observe how many people refuse to react to sound and logical suggestions for investment and yet who take immediate, and oftentimes sizable, positions in something which emanates from the flimsiest of sources. There is something about a whisper, something about a supposed secret, which converts a sensible Dr. Jekyll into an irrational Mr. Hyde.

I equate tips with chain letters. If you are at the top of the ladder you may be all right, but if you are on the lower rungs you had better face up to the fact that there is a crowd ahead of you which will know when to sell long before you do.

Closely related to tip-buying is the urge to take advantage of short-term developments such as special dividends, government contract awards, etc. As with tips, you are probably way down the line in the information network on such matters. One sensible practice is to avoid stocks which are considered because of temporary developments *unless you would be willing to buy them even if the hoped-for development did not take place.*

Another part of the tip syndrome is the fear of missing the boat. Is it hard to pass up that bargain counter at Macy's where items are marked down to fifty cents and where people are clamoring to buy something, anything! There may not be the slightest need for the item, but if others crave it, how can you pass it up? We discussed the dangerous supply-demand consequences of this in chapter 4.

Most of this easy-money problem is an extension of envy and a fear of being forced later to kick oneself in the pants. After all, if you pass up easy money, what a damned fool you are! An intelligent offset is to project the adage "Beware of Greeks bearing gifts" one step further and be willing to concentrate instead on slightly more arduous, but far more sensible, approaches to stock investing.

On to trading and gunslinging. To begin with, you should know that the former has *not* been the way riches have been built over the years and the latter involves a go-for-broke attitude which involves unnecessary risk-taking.

Both the trader and the gunslinger may well be hung up on a typical gambler's false sense of satisfaction from occasional victories. The inveterate gambler is the fellow who glories in one triumph, sometimes to the total exclusion of the many defeats he has encountered. The need to repeat such shallow victories is a symptom of psychological problems which vary from person to person and which can become highly involved. If you are one who revels in the joy of buying a stock at $40 and selling it three days later at $44, and if you need a constant barrage of such minor victories to keep you stimulated or happy, you had best discover right now that you are worshiping false idols. *Excitement for its own sake, or some flimsy definition of what it is to be "right," rather than substantial financial rewards, may have become your goal.*

Another possible driving force emanates from the common inferiority feeling already discussed. The need for constant small conquests may stem from *a desire to impress someone.* That someone could be just little old you (and your psyche); or it could be your wife (remember—that's bad Investual Relations), your pals, your stockbroker (yes, even that second-rate citizen) or even—brace yourself—the Internal Revenue Service.

Now we know that Rosenberg has flipped his lid. The Internal Revenue Service? Who in the world would want to make an impression on this monster?

Well, frankly I don't know. And actually I don't believe that it is the IRS itself which is the object. There *is,* however, something about making out that income-tax form—or reading what someone else has prepared for you—which is highly emotional. (Maybe it's simply your accountant you are trying to impress.) In other words, the capital-gains section is more or less an extension of that victory syndrome we discussed. Showing a series of pluses, it bolsters the ego and reminds us how smart we were during the year.

Personally I want to get my kicks elsewhere—not on my income-tax return. As a matter of fact, the ideal situation is to show *minimum* gains, perhaps even net losses, on your annual April 15 horror magazine *and to know that your assets have grown substantially over the period.* As you will soon learn, my philosophy is to let good stocks run, with the ultimate idea being to hold them and pay no tax at all. This is not to say that I am opposed to taking big profits; certainly not! But there is no sense in forcing this. After all, the measure of success should be the amount of *keepable* dollars of gain on an annual basis.

Anyway, for those of you who might have a "thing" going for the IRS, I should remind you that it has become highly computerized. Let me tell you —if impressing *machines* is your goal, forget the rest of this book and call for the men in the white jackets, *right now.*

More on the "Stock Strayer"

As long as I am criticizing the short-term trader, I should include one more psychological element which is not fully understood and which is injurious to proper investment technique. I am referring to a condition which encourages people to go from stock to stock, rather than limit themselves to less activity in fewer issues. Imagine if you will stock *A* which you have just purchased at forty dollars; within a short period, it rises to forty-four dollars, which in some people creates a need to take action. The origin of this need varies from person to person. For some the 10 percent gain is by definition the goal in mind—which is utterly ridiculous; after all, you will need an absolute bushelful of these, even without any losses, to hit the jackpot, especially after tax considerations. For others, the rise just creates nervousness (unlike us, they are not relaxed with their investments) and the only way out of this nervousness is to unload. And for others, the increase brings out a "the grass is always greener on the other side of the street" thought pattern. Yes, this stock strayer has experienced an emotional kick in seeing the stock move from forty to forty-four dollars and he wants to go on to another stock and accomplish the same thing again. The fact that stock *A* might go on from forty-four dollars to forty-eight or fifty or sixty dollars or anywhere is not as important as obtaining a new emotional charge. So out he goes of *A* and in he goes to *B. It might well be that* B *has just experienced a rise similar to that of* A, *but Sammy Strayer has not "felt" this emotion.*

This is one of the important reasons why people cannot stand prosperity and cannot stay around for *big* winners (chapter 20 will discuss this further). They start out by purchasing some stock, which, unless it is at its absolute bottom, was obviously owned by someone at a lower price; this does not inhibit the buyer, however, as he did not experience the previous emotion involved in seeing it rise. Then the stock climbs, he feels this emotion, and moves to another in which he has not yet had this feeling. This latter company may be *less* attractive than the one he has left, but that thought is obliterated by his programmed nervousness regarding stocks. And on and on he goes, until of course he purchases a stock which declines. Now he has a different problem.

At any rate, his flitting around really hasn't accomplished much for him—except for the kind of shallow victories already discussed. In this case, however, the reason behind the excessive trading stems from this little-discussed emotional hangup. In a way, this is like the lad who has to conquer a new lassie every week either to prove something to himself or to gain a fresh emotional experience. If he only realized that his old honey Miss Xerox is pretty solid and exciting and understanding herself, he wouldn't have to go through all the secretaries in the office and then go to the neighborhood bar and seek out a Miss Eastman or a Miss IBM—only to end up with dumpy old Miss Buggywhip.

The stock strayer likewise fails to understand the basic mathematics of speculation. Accomplished gamblers will tell you that the overlooked element of importance is the science of betting. For example, the poker player who waits for the good hands to bet is really gambling far less than the players who cannot resist the temptation to take a peek at each and every pot. The ones who draw to a pair of three's, literally praying that another three and a pair of kings will be dealt, are relying on miracles—and statistics do not favor miracles or those who hope for them. Stock buyers following the same principle will end up with depleted resources. Thus, you should not feel a compulsion to be fully invested at all times. Even if you anticipate a market rise, you should commit capital only when you feel reasonably confident of the prospects for a particular investment situation. Remember that there is always another day in the stock market and that each session brings its opportunities.

How Stock Brokers Encourage Straying

Incidentally, stock brokers are among the worst culprits in this "grass is always greener" pattern. During the time I headed a large research department in a brokerage concern, I constantly observed salesmen becoming enthusiastic about a recommended stock—only to turn themselves off the minute it experienced any sort of rise in price. All the reasoning in the world could not replace their emotional satisfaction. I would explain that the original suggestion was made with far higher goals than the small gain already realized and that the stock up 5 or 10 percent was still more attractive than anything else on the horizon at the moment. But the typical reaction was one of paralysis. While they might have found it difficult to vocalize their inner feelings, their actions showed they were feeling, "Give us something new—something in which we have not felt the excitement of a quick rise!"

The ticker tape itself contributes to this very problem. A person watching the parade of stock prices lives what seems to be a lifetime of stock fluctuations in a matter of days. Certainly this contributes to nervousness and anxiety on the part of the viewer—perhaps to the point where he actually believes he has owned a security much longer than he truly has.

Bah, Bah, Bah!

As might be expected, there is a personality group which reacts to this same set of circumstances in an opposite manner. Some investors, for example, react to rising prices much as the person described on page 122 who cannot resist that bargain counter at Macy's. While this case involves a higher, rather than a reduced, price, the magnet is similarly something which looks like it might be running away from him. If he is watching the ticker or observing closing prices in the newspaper the upward action creates a compelling urge to join the crowd. Whether this, too, is a fear of missing the boat or whether it is an extension of the human tendency to conform, the reaction is one of joining the flock *without consideration of other factors.*

Gambling for the Crucial

One final category of excessive trading stems from a desire on the part of some to improve on *crucial* goals already achieved. Contrary to the maxim of the bird in the hand, many people will risk comfortable goals already attainable, such as adequate retirement, a trip to Europe, a house, a car, etc. The money may already be there but either time burns a hole in their pocket or the zest for improving the kitty takes over—and the market becomes the vehicle for their new sights.

Remember that I am stressing the impropriety of risking *crucial* goals. It is one (serious) thing to play around and risk something which you want or need badly; it is another to invest for the future and for sensible goals. Stated more directly, if you have the dollars for the car of your dreams, buy it and do not gamble just because you know that a Rolls-Royce hums along a bit better and that you might just achieve that, too.

Aside from the wisdom of living for today, the person who plays with crucial money makes a bad investor. He is under great tension from the beginning and suffers from all the maladies associated with such tension. Thus, if your gambling in the market makes you nervous, realize that this alone may be your problem. As stated earlier, you should never risk your comfort and happiness.

The Use of Leverage

Leverage, which is simply a fancy word for "borrowing," carries a strange connotation when it comes to stock investing. Much of this no doubt emanates from the horrible experiences of 1929, wherein people had been allowed to borrow 90 percent of their stock purchases and where only a moderate decline wiped them out.

Frankly, no stigma should exist against borrowing to buy stocks, any more than to make real estate, business, or consumer purchases. As mentioned, stocks should represent good companies operating in good industries, and so long as this is the case I see no reason why an investor should not use borrowed money.

The problem obviously revolves around the question of *how much*. And while the answer varies from person to person, depending on circumstances and on the relative state of the stock market, the word "margin" should be no more of an ogre than "mortgage" or "installment debt."

The fact is, however, that many of the problem elements being described in this book entice people into overuse of leverage in the stock market. Certainly ego is a major culprit, as is greed; likewise, envy, a quest for excitement, and a fear of missing the boat. We have already seen that such psychological tendencies, unbridled, lead to many problems.

The solution lies in knowing oneself and in having the important pieces in place; in a sensible plan which avoids excess; in short, in a Psycho-Cybernetic approach. In a way, it is similar to the avoidance of black-and-white thinking. I consider it less risky to be leveraged in a good stock than pay all cash for a weak one—once again all within the limits of sound judgment.

The Gunslinger

The chapter has concentrated mainly on the active trader, to the neglect of the gunslinger. Actually, the gunslinger is an operator made up of two parts. The first part is the trader already described. The second part is the go-for-broke gambler—the kind who believes that his innate brilliance has made his risk minimal. He is willing to buy any kind of security for almost any kind of account simply because he is convinced that he is infinitely smarter than the rest of the investing crowd. His ego has run away with him to the point where he believes he can outwit others merely by a constant barrage of buys and sells. As in so many other fields, the gunslinger suffers from pressing too hard. Despite his conviction to the contrary, there is no ultimate wisdom in stock investing; and there is no need for a hell-bent-for-leather approach. You can make money—and plenty of it—without a kamikaze effort. Something in between the tortoise and the hare is what has worked for me and for many others, and such a happy medium has weathered the storms of time.

Conclusions

The compulsive trader and the gunslinger can benefit from the thought presented in chapter 7. By realizing that stocks are not mere pieces of paper to be shuffled indiscriminately and that they instead represent living entities—presumably sound businesses with strong assets and imaginative leadership—the input is strengthened considerably. Both economic success and serenity should result as a consequence.

The importance of this whole discussion is that it provides you with an understanding of the gambling instinct. To be successful in the stock market, you must recognize such tendencies in yourself and in others and know how to react to them. You must spot nervousness which is obliterating logic and good judgment.

Our Psycho-Cybernetic approach is to isolate personality tendencies and to enhance the right ones and reduce those which breed trouble. This is a starting point for self-improvement. Coincident with this is the replacement of negative and restrictive inputs with constructive ones—something which this particular discussion should have accomplished.

14. Popeye, The Sailor Man

One of the great cartoon characters of all times is, of course, Popeye. Now one can safely say that, other than spinach and Olive Oyl, Popeye's saving grace was a great set of muscles. As a matter of fact (and no offense to Popeye lovers), brute force was Popeye's salvation; he really did not possess anything startling "upstairs" and he generally got himself into one heck of a pickle prior to the spinach infusion. In a way Popeye had what is known today as "tunnel vision" in that he knew only one way to extricate himself from trouble—force.

Assuming Popeye had some semblance of the

power to reason and that we could expose him to Psycho-Cybernetics, he could certainly be helped. You see, one of Popeye's problems stemmed from a constant piece of data input which only reinforced his tunnel vision. I refer to the fact that before and after every episode he would sing his own song, which contained the phrase, "I am what I am, That's all that I am, I'm Popeye the Sailor Man" (toot-toot). Sure, he ate all his spinach and fought till the finish —but, by God, he wasn't about to change. He was what he was and that's all that he was—and anyone who wanted him to be otherwise had just better steer clear 'cause he (Popeye) might just knock him right out of sight.

Do you know that there are "Popeye investors" —and an absolute plethora of them? Investors who believe they can muscle their way to stock-market success and who have the same tunnel vision concerning their own personalities, abilities, and capabilities that Popeye does? Such individuals have not recognized that success in investing parallels success in other avenues of life in that you will achieve much more and far more easily if:

1. You know yourself;
2. You learn to compensate for inherent weaknesses while at the same time striving to put your greatest strengths to work; and
3. You open your mind to self-improvement.

Please note that I avoid a plea for forcing yourself to invest *contrary to your nature.* But this does not mean you should take a "I am what I am, That's all that I am" attitude either. Said another way, you can take one of two approaches to your investing. You can invest only within your present personality structure, in which case you will experience a minimum of tension—but most probably a minimum of success. Or you can follow a Psycho-Cybernetic tack and at least try to compensate for an idiosyncrasy here and there.

Let us begin with my "depression-affluence" theory on investors, which asserts that the attitude people have towards stocks is based on age and exposure. Generalizing very broadly, it stands to reason that people have developed investment tendencies which relate to the most important experiences of their lives. For example, it is no wonder that the person who lost all his chips in 1929 and/or who witnessed people standing in breadlines in the 1930s has some negative input concerning investing which has become part of his personality. By the same token, the person born in 1950 has no idea of what business depression is all about. He has never lived when things were really rough and, probably being a part of the affluent society, he thinks of business and the economy as a smoothly paved one-way road. (This may have been altered by the 1970 recession–stock-market crash.)

Admitting that there are countless exceptions, you should at least think about your own age and exposure and wonder whether you fit a very general pattern such as the following: if you are over fifty, no one has to remind you that you lived through 1929 and really observed and felt the depression of the 1930s—something which might have left a real scar; if you are over thirty-five, but under fifty, you are an indirect product of the depression (you grew up in it, felt it more indirectly, but probably did not suffer from the very worst of it); and if you are fortunate enough to be much under thirty-five, you are a product of the Affluent Society (and probably were brought up in a more permissive environment, too).

The emotional tendencies resulting from the above are quite obvious. The first group has most reason for fear and has more reason for thinking in terms of bonds, savings accounts, etc. The second group rests somewhere between this and the latter, which harbors more of the gunslinging, equity-oriented, risk-taking personalities (I speak solely in terms of the stock market, that is). You ought, therefore, to think about where you fit in this scheme and determine whether you need to alter the related input to any extent.

More pertinent to our discussion is the willingness on the part of the investor to analyze, as well as possible, his own broad temperament and personality characteristics, without regard to age or exposure. For example, I would suggest that you ask yourself whether you are

Self-assured	or	Lacking confidence
Relaxed	or	Nervous
Placid	or	Emotional
Progressive	or	Ultraconservative
Skeptical	or	Gullible
Patient	or	Impatient
Positive	or	Negative
Organized	or	Disorganized

It must be obvious that certain of the above traits are bound to be to your advantage in your investment procedures. You should be confident, for example, provided that you have developed a sound philosophy and an informed approach. You should be relaxed with your investments and unemotional about them. You should be skeptical enough to resist the ridiculous stories you hear and yet be positive enough (yes, even an optimist by nature) that you can see the bright side of life and potential investment opportunities. And you should be organized in your approach and be patient with those stocks you have bought for the right reasons. Just as the Boy Scouts have their oath which tells them they should be trustworthy, loyal, helpful, friendly, courteous, kind, obedient, cheerful, thrifty, brave, clean, and reverent, an investor should have his own oath which mirrors his proper characteristics.

Come to think of it, the inputs suggested thus far haven't done badly in building an arsenal of important and useful traits. Constructing a good investor's oath from what we have offered would provide us with: a good investor is logical, disciplined, positive-thinking, enthusiastic, and relaxed with his stock choices and with his stock ownership. Add imaginative and patient (both of which will be discussed in later chapters) to the above and you have a fair dictum for yourself. Relative to little ole you personally, you should in addition look to an analysis of your other personal idiosyncrasies—such as the checklist provided on page 136. No Popeye you, the next step is to isolate those characteristics which have a negative bearing on your investing, with an eye to improvement or adjustment. An autosuggestion (self-talk) approach to these is ideal. Or, if you are the type who has no interest in this design, at least make sure the person advising you is aware of the hangups. Perhaps he can compensate for them for you, if you give him a chance.

To ensure your tackling the problem in some way, I have constructed a short questionnaire which will help you rate yourself. Before proceeding, answer whether your investment objective is:

a. Solely for dividends and current income.

b. Solely for capital appreciation.

c. For a combination of income and capital gains.

If your answer is *a* the rest of the questions may be unnecessary. Be sure, however, that you really do need the income you are seeking; many times people think they do but in reality have what they require and instead are merely putting a lot of income dollars right back into the savings bank. The most successful investors are those who do not reach for that last bit of income and instead invest in companies which may pay them much more over the years through both steadily rising dividends and through capital appreciation. At any rate, if your answer is either *b* or *c* read on.

INVESTOR QUESTIONNAIRE

1. Investment Goals and Current Position

With regard to assets and income, I

a. Will have to hit some big winners to reach my goals;

b. Should be able to accumulate all I need without straining;

c. Already have pretty much all I require or will ever require.

When investing for capital gains, I

a. Set my sights on short-term gains;

b. Invest for the very long term (i.e., 5–10 years);
c. Aim for intermediate-term gains (i.e., 1–5 years).

2. Investment Reactions

a. I think the country is going to hell.
b. I see nothing but growth for the U.S. economy.
c. I think the nation has great strengths but realize that it will have its ups and downs.

a. I am frightened of the stock market.
b. I see the market as a game.
c. I believe the market holds great potential but only with an organized approach.

a. I never sell what I buy.
b. I look to sell soon after I buy.
c. I only sell when fundamentals (of the economy, the market, or the company) change.

a. I tend to keep my losers.
b. I tend to sell losers very late.
c. I tend to sell losers early.

a. I tend to sell my winners early.
b. I tend not to sell my winners.
c. I tend to sell when it appears as if the outlook is changed.

a. I consider myself basically unlucky.
b. I consider myself reasonably lucky.
c. I consider myself a person who can create his own good fortune.

While admittedly general, your responses will tell you something about yourself. For the eight questions posed, give yourself one for each *a* answer, two for *b*, and three for *c*. Be honest—you are only hurting yourself if you fudge. You no doubt noted the pattern as you progressed through the inquiries. The higher the score the better your chances for stock-market success.

In the section on Investment Goals and Current Position, the better answers are either *b* or *c* to both questions, with *c* being best. If *a* was your answer on the first, then you still have hope if *b* or *c* were your responses to the second.

In the Investment Reactions part, if you do not register a minimum of thirteen points, you face an uphill battle in the stock market. Perhaps the balance of this book will help you out, but you had better come back after finishing and take the exam again.

Equally important, make sure your broker or adviser is aware of your responses on this questionnaire. A good broker will serve to neutralize weak traits; if he cannot, perhaps he harbors them himself. As a matter of fact, some of the questionnaire can be posed to him—i.e., the second query of the first section; and the first, third, fourth, and fifth parts of the second group. Make sure he gets high marks, too.

The Element of Ego in Investing

Thus far the only direct mention of the powerful term "ego" occurred in our discussion of gambling and gunslinging in the stock market. Certainly this is not to imply that ego is solely the property of this one group of investors. Indeed, ego is a potential driving force for all of us and it is important to understand this if we are to "un-Popeye" our investment reactions.

One of the most respected economists of all times is the renowned Lord John Maynard Keynes—a person who not only understood economic theories but who made himself a fortune in common stocks. In his famous work, *The General Theory of Employment, Money and Interest,* Keynes points to ego as the most powerful influence on human action generally and as the basis for understanding the all-important emotional influences in the stock market. According to Keynes, investing for profit goes beyond the mere desire for financial gains. "The actual, private object of the most skilled investor today is 'to beat the gun,' . . . to outwit the crowd." He goes on to compare the battle of wits to the childhood games of Old Maid or Musical Chairs, where the victor delights in slipping the old maid to his neighbor before the game is over or in grabbing a chair for himself when the music stops. Alas, it is simply the quest to prevail at the expense of others.

Naturally it is important for you to realize that such ego may well be the derivation for others' actions in the market, but most important you must become aware of this very tendency yourself—if you have it. Thus, you should ask yourself just why you are involved in stock investing. Maybe it is for sound financial reasons, but maybe it is for gratifications which go way beyond dollars and cents.

Are you buying stocks to prove something? Are you holding on to stocks when you know you shouldn't merely because the realized loss would constitute admission of defeat and inferiority? Are you nervous or tense because of deep emotional involvements?

None of this is for me to determine. I am neither a trained psychologist or psychiatrist. But I have observed more than fifteen years of strange investor behavior—much of which is the basis for this book. The value to you is the recognition of ego and the understanding that its existence to the exclusion of common sense and good judgment is one important reason for the general lack of success which investors experience. Frankly, a diminution of ego is a necessity for many investors if they are to achieve economic rewards and serenity.

Conclusions

Unless you possess a supply of greens which will serve as Popeye's spinach did or unless you have an Olive Oyl of your very own, a self-analysis such as the questionnaire demands and an understanding of your personality, temperament, ego, and other characteristics as described in the chapter is essential for your success in the stock market. This, combined with positive self-talk, can create an attitude which will justify a vastly improved self-image. Remember—you are what you are, but that isn't all you have to be. Right? *Right!*

15. All That Glitters . . .

There is nothing like approaching a column, an article, or a chapter in a book where you know right from the start that some of your readers are going to be alienated and insulted as a result of your efforts. Certainly a number of my chapters carry these very risks, but then any work which hits people where they live holds such dangers. Perhaps it is only for my own therapy that I point up this fact of life; after all, if you turn off 5 percent of your readers in each of twenty chapters, you finally wipe out all of them—not the happiest of prospects for the fellow slaving away to make a success of what he is doing.

Like the umpire in baseball, however, my aim is to call 'em as I see 'em—and frankly when we come to the subject of gold and gold buyers* and gold "wishers" I might as well warn you that I see a psychological pattern which is hardly pleasant.

Starting out with the metal itself, I am as cognizant as the next person as to gold's usefulness. It is a precious metal, highly malleable and ductile, which does not rust; it has constituted the basis for monetary exchange throughout the world for centuries; and it possesses great beauty and makes damn fine jewelry. Furthermore, writers of such magnitude as Chaucer, Cervantes, Dryden, and Shakespeare have thought enough of it to use it as a basis of comparison for anything which might look to be shiny and beautiful and valuable. As they say, all that glitters is not gold.

But, alas, eager investors, that which has glittered in monetary value over the past few decades has not been gold at all. During years in which inflation has been the order of the day throughout the world, and real-estate values and stock prices have skyrocketed, the price of gold has remained constant; its official U.S. price was raised from $20.67 per fine ounce to $35.00 in 1933 and that is where it stood in December, 1970. As might be expected, investment in most gold-mining equities has been ex-

*As a U.S. citizen you are forbidden from owning gold itself for other than manufacturing or scientific reasons. Therefore, when I talk about the gold buyer I am referring to one who seeks refuge in gold through companies predominantly involved in such ownership (owning or controlling reserves, mining, etc.).

tremely disappointing over this period.

Actually, any detailed discussion of gold entails a very complicated explanation of the whole international monetary structure—something which is unnecessary here. Suffice it to say that gold, as mentioned, has not been a participant in the economic boom which has taken place in this nation since the end of World War II. And that any glamorous prospects from here would depend on either a loss of confidence in the U.S. dollar on the part of other countries or on a drastic need to stimulate the U.S. economy (such as the depression of the 1930s).

Stated very simply, gold as an investment for the U.S. citizen is for the person who feels the need for a hedge against *de*flation or for the person who believes that earnings are going to hell (the theory being that gold profits will at least hold even during such a period and, most important, that a hike in the price of the metal will have to be declared). Gold is for the individual who anticipates a world financial crisis or who lacks confidence in the dollar and in securities tied to the dollar.

The thesis of this chapter must be apparent—that the person who is attracted to gold as an investment might have some personality patterns which revolve around negativism and fear.*

My experiences over the years verify this prognosis—and every discussion I have had with other experienced people in the field confirms the view.

*Once again, this discussion pertains to the U.S. investor. It does not necessarily apply to the sophisticated hoarder overseas who can switch freely from shares into gold or the other way around, based on temporary conditions.

Some investors have very legitimate reasons for leaning towards gold. Perhaps they were wiped out in equities in 1929; or they recall the increase in the price of gold which took place in 1933 and which made gold stocks among the few which held their value during those depressed and depressing years; or some clamity, such as the oppression of Hitlerism, befell them which put a premium on owning something precious which could be transported easily when fleeing a country.

Psycho-Cybernetics fosters empathy and we should have compassion for those who have experienced such disasters in their lives or who fear them. Others who wish for gold seem to fall into one of the following categories:

1. The person who has had the majority of his money in cash for years and who is fearful that a plunge into equities at this moment will be ill timed. He has seen others prosper in stocks for years and is afraid that, "just my luck," the cycle will change after he has finally become involved (this is a little bit of chapter 11, "On Kicking Oneself in the Pants").
2. The individual who has been envious of others' successes in business or the stock market for years and who realizes that success in gold probably means problems for them.
3. The sadistic person who gets his kicks from reveling in others' misfortunes.
4. The extra-nervous investor who wants to hedge himself against every conceivable disaster (which he probably pictures in his mind on a nonstop basis).

I could go on conjecturing how and why the

typical gold buyer or gold-price "wisher" thinks and behaves as he does. Actually, the subject is probably deep enough to deserve a thorough study of its own.

From our standpoint, all that is necessary is to:

a. Realize that the gold "wish" invades the stock market every so often—and usually in a very vocal manner. By understanding the possible genesis of such thinking, you will be able to withstand the pressures that are generated; and

b. Recognize the basic tendencies of gold fever and do something about them if they apply to you. These characteristics are naturally going to inhibit a person in normal money-making endeavors, whether it be business, real estate, or stocks.

For years I have argued against those who have predicted gold-price increases and who have recommended ownership of gold stocks. Frankly, I now see signs that a price increase might be justified once again—but not for the negative, "tonic" reasons normally heard. It so happens that private demand for the metal continues; and that, with the exception of new mining in South Africa, output of gold is declining. If inflation continues in other commodities, gold might simply become too cheap (relatively) and a higher price might finally develop.

Despite this possibility, gold is hardly a reasonable choice for consistent growth of capital. Most important, as already stressed, just be sure that any enthusiasm generated for it is not the product of basic negativism or desire for the destruction of others. There is an expression that "gold is where you find it." Generally speaking, this optimistic statement should evolve from a constructive approach to life such as Psycho-Cybernetics. From an investment standpoint, the glitter should emanate not from sinking dollars into the metal itself, but from an overview and philosophy such as *Psycho-Cybernetics and the Stock Market.*

16. Things Are Going To Hell

I am the first to admit that the big things going on around us these days are hardly the most encouraging that could be imagined. Pick up the morning newspaper or turn on the radio or TV for the headline news and the subjects range from war in Vietnam to starvation somewhere to protests in schools; and to dope and crime and all types of lovely little happenings which are enough to take the optimistic stuffing out of anyone.

The reaction to this kind of news and events is often summed up in the title of this chapter—things are going to hell—something which has a decided bearing on our daily attitudes and, you guessed it, on any efforts we might make in the world of investments. In a nutshell, a statement like "Things are going to hell" hardly encourages smiles, bounce in your walk, or general overall happiness; and the pessimism it suggests hardly creates the ideal climate for stock investing. The fearful attitude which it generates fosters the type of tension and worry which we have already identified as being detrimental to good habits.

While there is no denying the discouraging events, it is important to realize that they often become exaggerated. The fact is that each age has its crises which, *at the time, look to be worse than anything until then.* Indeed, things looked like they were going to hell in practically every year of every decade—in some way. If you don't believe me, think back over the past four decades. The 1930s were certainly no jewel, what with hunger, unemployment and all-out depression; and with the atrocities of Adolf Hitler and the ominous world tensions. Then came the 1940s, more than half of which was spent in actual worldwide conflict, with millions of casualties, property devastated, and all the horrors associated with such a war. The 1950s had Korea and McCarthyism, continuous conflict with the Russians, and fears about so many things. And the 1960s had Vietnam and the Kennedy assassinations and protests against almost everything (much of it deserved, of course).

So really—when you look back—are the things which are going to hell today that much worse than before? Have we lost sight of the fact that more of our population is eating well and living better than ever before? And have we neglected to realize that ferment is often necessary to alter the defects of a society? What we perceive—and the opinions we derive—depends to a great extent on our frame of reference. Like the identical twins who grew up to be six feet tall, but with different personalities; one considered himself "the tallest midget in the world" and the other thought himself "the shortest giant." Or like two people contemplating the same half-filled glass; the optimist sees it as half full while the pessimist views it as half empty!

Or like the people who play with statistics—for example, the figures on employment and unemployment in the U.S. With population expanding, odds favor the total number of people both employed and unemployed rising over a period of time. Thus, if you started with a theoretical 4 million persons unemployed out of a total of 100 million employable in a given year, for a 4 percent unemployment rate, you obviously would have made some progress if, ten years later, with the population up to 150 million, the number of unemployed increased to 5 million, or 3.3 percent of the total. You can be sure, however, that some pessimists would be quick to emphasize the 5 million figure alone and not think in terms of all-important relative values. Instead, they might conclude that, once again, "Things are going to hell."

The Role of the Press

Contributory to this thought process is the typical role of the press anywhere. As they say, dog bites man is hardly news. But find a story of man bites dog and you have potential front-page material. With all due respect to the newspapers and to those who produce them, a person assessing his own moods and reactions should remember that startling, sensational stories sell more copies—and it is easier to find such sensationalism relating to the negative than to the positive.

Needless to say, there are countless reasons why we as individuals tend to have our morale diminished. The important thing is to see things within proper perspective—with a framework of reference which allows some sunlight to filter through what might be a dark and overpowering cloud.

She Ain't What She Used to Be

Quite similar to the "Things are going to hell" thought pattern—and equally destructive—is what I call the "Old Gray Mare" syndrome, which emphasizes that things "ain't what they used to be." A good example of this is the photo I observed one day in the sports section of a large newspaper; it showed a couple of survivors of a great football team of the past—and it centered on their comments about the game today, which they thought to be vastly inferior to that played when they cavorted on the gridiron. No, by cracky, things weren't as they used to be! Not like the good old days! Of course today's linemen tilt the scales at a measly 240 versus around 180 dripping wet in the old days; and today the finesse of passes, draw plays, red dogs, multiple offenses, and the like have brought more science and cunning to the game than ever before. And milers are breaking four minutes regularly and pole vaulters are clearing seventeen feet. And swimmers are swimming faster and basketball players are hitting the hoop with far greater accuracy. But no, football ain't what it used to be. Not much!

Alas, whether it be sports or business or what have you, the chances are very good that things are a whale of a lot better today than they used to be. Once we are able to separate out our nostalgia for the past, I think we will agree that this is the case.

On Nostalgia

Speaking of nostalgia, positive thinkers make the practical suggestion that you create instead a "forward look" and *develop a nostalgia for the future rather than for the past.* This approach is far more youthful; and it provides you with direction—with all-important *goals*—all of which constitute the key to a success-type personality.

The Case of K. P. Tsolainos

One excellent illustration of how all this relates to stock investing emanates from an experience of mine in June, 1962. Now if your memory does not serve you correctly, the year 1962 was one of considerable weakness in the stock market. To be blunt, it fell smack out of bed, partly because an adjustment was necessary as a result of some great excesses which built up in 1961 and partly because investors were worried about business generally and about the Administration's attitude towards profits (remember the confrontation between U.S. Steel's Mr. Blough and President Kennedy?). As 1962 progressed, prices slid lower and lower—and then, as is typical of bear markets, the sliding turned to plummeting.

On one June day of that year, my firm J. Barth & Co. had arranged for a luncheon honoring Mr. K. P. Tsolainos, who was the senior partner of a fine New York firm, Baker, Weeks & Co. Little did we know when we planned the luncheon, which included many of Barth's registered representatives, that the market would break by about twenty points on the very day of this affair. In short, the mood was dismal and the luncheon took on the characteristics of a post-funereal gathering. Yes, things were actually going to hell!

Mr. Tsolainos was a tiny man in his seventies, with a slight accent and without any unusual abilities as a speaker. He had emigrated to the United States from Greece at a very early age and had started his Wall Street career running errands and doing the most menial tasks. He had risen to an important position, but he hardly looked to possess the stature or the personality to bring this particular crowd out of its funk.

After dessert had been served, Barth's senior partner, Marco F. Hellman, made an appropriate introduction and the next thing we knew "K. P."was on his feet addressing this half-depressed group. "Gosh," I thought, "I hope he'll give us some new stock ideas—some which might hold promise for going up, not down." That's what we needed: new and fresh ideas.

Well, you know what? K. P. didn't give us one stock to think about; not even one. And yet he made a speech which was far more practical and useful than if he had provided us with a dozen ideas.

For the next twenty minutes, K. P. Tsolainos, Greek emigrant, really told us what it was all about. That things might appear to be going to hell, but that, in proper perspective, they were not at all. That this great country of ours was a land of opportunity for him some fifty years earlier and that he felt that it offered the same—no, even greater—opportunity today. Yes, today—which was then June, 1962—at a moment which looked like a veritable end to much of what we had counted on and expected from our society.

Sure, K. P. was flag-waving. And sure, he was emotional and prejudiced because of his own experiences. But what he said made sense. Most of us were losing perspective and were letting this interfere with basic good judgment. Things were not going to hell after all.

Certainly it was coincidental that K. P.'s luncheon occurred on what later proved to be the bottom of the market—at a buying opportunity which was most unusual. His words represented a port of positive thinking in what was an ominous storm of destructive thought. And while it would be foolhardy to say that his confidence will be borne out forever, not that much has changed between 1962 and 1970 to have negated the fundamentals of his philosophy. So —while we are bound to witness recessions and all types of upsets in this country, chances are that they will be short lived which means that *just when everyone around you has reached the point of extreme negativism and depression is the most appropriate time for you to emulate K. P. Tsolainos.*

Some Psycho-Cybernetic self-talk which concentrates on K. P.'s philosophy is bound to make you a happier citizen as well as strengthening your investment armor. Something like: "I recognize the good things around me and concentrate on constructive goals" is definitely a vast improvement over any kind of "things are going to hell" or "things just aren't the way they used to be" doctrine. As mentioned, the greatest investment opportunities present themselves when conditions actually appear gloomy and when human beings have overreacted to the bleak prospect. Your ability to keep perspective during such times is essential. By doing so, you will be emulating Bernard Baruch's valuable advice on the wisdom of buying straw hats in the winter (when the prices are the lowest); and of " buying sheep and selling deer" (buy what looks shabby and sell what looks beautiful).

Finally, do not lose sight of the thought process which is useful in meeting any dilemma in life—that of projecting *what the alternative might be.*

In the case of investments, a person has the choice of a variety of vehicles, ranging from savings accounts to bonds to real estate and mortgages to business and self-employment to common stocks. Do not forget that a negative outlook concerning the latter generally has a similarly destructive effect on other vehicles as well. While these effects may not be as apparent as in stocks because of the fishbowl publicity already described, and while the order of magnitude is never going to be completely similar, there is generally some parallel.

In addition, you should remind yourself that there is always a huge pool of capital looking for a good rate of return—and that this is worldwide. This money is constantly seeking a profitable home and it has, as part of its consideration, a responsibility of stability. Thus, you might be able to earn 20 to 30 percent per year in Brazilian bonds but if you awaken one day to learn that the country's cruzeiro has been devalued once again your net return will be small—or perhaps nothing at all. Or if you are concerned over inflation here in the U.S. you should remind yourself that it is not exactly nonexistent abroad.

In a nutshell, we tend to magnify our problems and oftentimes forget that they may not be so bad relative to those of other nations. Carrying this still further, recall that considerable quantities of investable funds from throughout the world have little choice but to funnel eventually to our markets—provided, of course, that our conditions do not deteriorate significantly.

If you do get down in the dumps, therefore, *be sure to consider the alternatives facing others seeking investments which offer some semblance of stability along with desired rates of return.*

17. A Chicken In Every Pot

Now that I have, I hope, convinced you that things are not going straight to hell, I will resort to typical stock-market *modus operandi* and talk out of the opposite side of my mouth by insisting that a fantastic new era is not around the corner, either. It may be true that we in the United States are a good deal closer to Herbert Hoover's promise of a chicken in every pot and a car in every garage, but Golden Years—without severe problems—are tough to come by. Even with very favorable demographic trends existing and with the federal government, regardless of political party, committed to huge spending, prosperity is bound to be erratic.

To be extra successful in the stock market, it is imperative to understand this simple fact and to develop a mental attitude which affords you the flexibility to anticipate these inevitable business peaks and troughs. Whereas thus far I have emphasized positive thought patterns, the ideal investor attitude is what I term "enthusiastic skepticism." The first of these two words, "enthusiastic," emanates from having confidence, from being imaginative and creative, from developing farsightedness, from understanding the emotions of both yourself and others, and from being a goal-oriented individual—all of which either have been or will be covered by this book. The second word, "skepticism," acts as a balance; it is the defense against gullibility (and is there ever plenty of this around!) and it is the weight which *turns enthusiasm into objectivity.* Just as certain great performing artists have the ability to generate laughter and then pathos, the ideal investor is one who can balance enthusiasm and skepticism. Emotional balance such as this leads to far superior control over one's investment destiny.

A Lesson on Cycles

One reason this controlled mental attitude is necessary stems from the inevitability of business interruptions. Actually the crux of the matter lies in the very significant fact that *an economy is made up of human beings*—people who have considerable self-interest and who cannot be relied upon to control themselves relative to wages, prices, and expansion. Adults are little more than grown-up children, and you can no more expect a businessman or a laborer to limit himself in his quest for the buck than you would a two-year-old who has just discovered the cookie jar to stop after consuming the first one. In addition, people have a tendency to overextend themselves. Create the right psychology and make the funds available and consumers will spend themselves into great debt. Create the right business climate and the board of directors of Consolidated Hula Hoops will be prone to participate in the action of the moment, yielding to the temptation to build bigger plants to produce more and more hoops, even though demand might be pretty well saturated. In other words, *it is naive to think that people will restrain themselves so that the economy will avoid occasional overheating and potential inflationary trends.* And since the faster you overexpand and inflate the worse the correction period is, the conclusion is that human beings left to themselves will ultimately overindulge themselves into real economic sickness and hangover. Certainly the experiences of the United States and every other major economy of the world bear this out—the result of which has been the establishment of outside bodies whose purpose is to even out the feasts and famines which would result without their influences.

So you see that my analysis of economic motivations is nothing individual to me nor is it a startling discovery. Business and government have realized, too, that men cannot be left to their own desires so far as spending, production, planning, etc., are concerned.

To illustrate, the United States has its Federal Reserve Board (FRB), whose major responsibility it is to act as an economic pacemaker by regulating the flow of money throughout the banking system. Through controlling discount rates, bank reserve requirements, stock-market margin regulations, and through open-market activities in the buying and selling of government obligations, the FRB holds the throttle of the economy. Fortunately in this nation, the FRB is a nonpolitical body and as such can (theoretically at least) pursue unpopular measures to hold down over-enthusiasm—which is what it has done and will no doubt continue to do in the future.

In general the FRB has taken the approach that it is a better policy to nip a business boom in the bud and thereby even risk recession than to wear blinkers and allow natural excesses to take place—which, once exhausted, might lead to another depression.

Ideally, of course, the FRB would like to run the economy like an automobile going a moderate and pleasant thirty-five miles per hour, with minimum pressure on either the brake or the accelerator.

While it attempts to do just this, the problem of dealing with a mass of complex, changing human beings complicates the situation. If only a slight tightening of credit and money supply would sober consumers, businessmen, and labor alike, then the FRB would have a relatively easy job—which it does not. Generally the population needs a klop on the head to bring it to its senses, which means having to tighten the screws more and more—until finally a mini-recession or some such adjustment period follows. When the pressure is finally eased, the mood of the populace is generally such that the former enthusiasm is difficult to regenerate. Just as the tightening could not be controlled so as to create a gradual dampening, the loosening usually has a delayed reaction, too. Thus, trying to regulate an economy is anything but an exact science.

All of this should be enough to convince you that new-era thinking is somewhat naïve. Despite promises from politicians and economic theorists, we *will* have our ups and downs. Needless to say, the stock market (which is sensitive to business jiggles) is bound to have similar, if not more violent, reactions.

Ideally, an investor should be conditioned to roll with the punches and take advantage of the inevitable fluctuations. If, therefore, you are the personality type which tends to get so embroiled with what is happening at the moment that you cannot see what lies beyond, you had better work hard on such emotionalism to place the same kind of governor on it that the FRB has on the economy. In other words, realize that even if we do get that car in every garage and chicken in every pot, the conditions may well stem from the facts that:

1. The car is there mainly because the consumer can hock himself to the eyeballs in debt to purchase it; and
2. The chicken is probably there because of that kind, bearded fellow, Colonel Sanders!!

Cycles Within Cycles

The lesson of this chapter may not have required all the space it took. There was method in my madness, however, as the ideas presented go beyond making you a skeptical security analyst and beyond warning you to be suspicious of promises for a steadily advancing economy. Most important, the lesson conditions you to the need for zigging and zagging in the vast majority of stocks in the market—an approach which requires extra sophistication and some fine tuning in your thought processes.

It should be unnecessary for me to state that this zigging and zagging has nothing to do with day-to-day trading; certainly chapter 13 ("The Folly of Gambling in the Stock Market") should have made my position clear on this. The fact is, however, that the majority of stocks require flexibility; to gain proper returns on them, you will have to consider both purchase *and* sale.

The Industry Strength Guide (pages 57–58) is a help in this thinking process as it sets out (1) those industry groups which are directly sensitive to the business cycle and which naturally require flexibility according to your opinion of the cycle; (2) those industries which are cyclical unto themselves; that is, they have their ups and downs, but these gyrations are usually separate from those of the general economy. This group likewise demands real flexibility; and (3) those which are, for the most part, not sensitive to cycles at all.

The first two categories are obvious zigzag areas—but the fact is that many of the apparently comfortable third group require change, too. *Either their seemingly stable businesses experience some interruptions or the stock market itself takes them to such extremes that they get way ahead of or way below what their real worth is.*

So now we get to the meat of the problem—which involves understanding how business generally operates in a free-enterprise society and in knowing how the stock market usually reacts to such a set of circumstances.

In *The Common Sense Way to Stock Market Profits* a chapter entitled "How to Avoid Fad Investments" presented what I deem to be as important as anything you can read relating to common-stock investing. The chapter mentioned is short (five pages) and yet it explains these all-important facts of life about business and related market psychology. As such, it provides an investor with a discipline and an ability to cope with problems. Let me point your attention to an illustration (on page 166) which was the heart of that discussion and ask you to glance over the words *on top* of the jagged line. These six stages explain how *business* in a competitive economy functions, even in such glamorous industries as computers, synthetic fibers, plastics, semiconductors, and a host of new-era wonderlands. Please study the pattern over again.

Alas, businessmen are human, too. As such, they tend to get wrapped up in the enthusiasm of their own involvements or that of their competitors and push ahead faster than they should. Or they simply are willing to plan way ahead for their expansion—at least much further ahead than the stock market

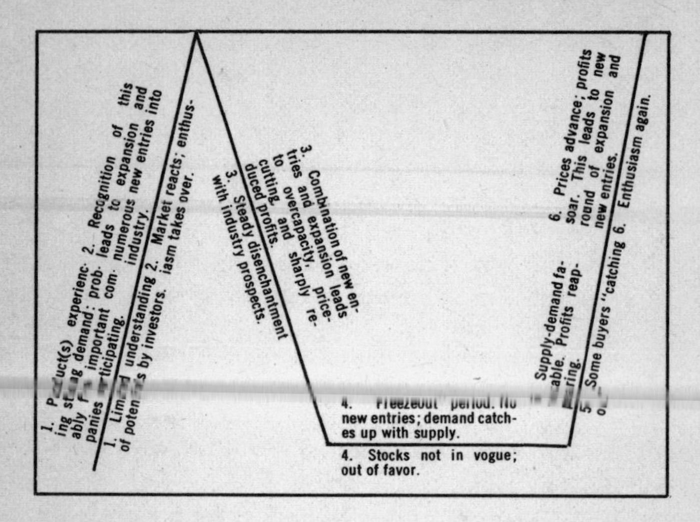

has patience for. The important realization is that an exceptionally glamorous area always attracts competition and that competition almost always leads to excess of supply over demand, which leads to price cutting and profit deterioration. Thus the business becomes, at least temporarily, less attractive, and it will take time for the men to be separated from the boys and for lush profits to appear again.

Now, please read the words *below* the line on the illustration. This signifies how the *stock market* typically reacts to this six-stage pattern of business behavior.

What stands out to you?

That the market is oblivious, negative, or disenchanted just when profits are ready to erupt—and enthusiastic as all get out just when things are getting ready to fall apart at the seams? If that strikes you,

you have read the chart correctly and you now understand just how and why people zig when they should zag and vice versa.

So—there are broad overall economic cycles to consider. And there are cycles within cycles. It is essential for you to understand this business behavior and to be able to anticipate the cycles stock-market-wise. In short, you must have the ability to control your emotions and to see conditions objectively enough so that you are a buyer at stages 1 and 4 and early 5 on our chart and a seller at late 2, early 3, or 6—not the opposite, as the huge majority are. In this way, you will avoid the huddling instinct we discussed as being so perilous in chapter 4. The combination of this understanding plus the Industry Strength Guide will place New Era-ism, Alice in Wonderland, Contrary Opinion, and other important thought processes in their proper perspective. As a result, you will not merely be a crowd follower and, as such, will be a significantly more polished investor.

Help from the Stock Brokers Plus More on Bah, Bah, Bahing!

Whereas there are, of course, many fine stock brokers as individuals and many fine brokerage firms, an objective appraisal leads one to the conclusion that the brokerage community itself contributes very much to the zigging-when-you-should-be-zagging process. To begin with, brokers—and the research forces behind them—are human and, as such, suffer from the same restrictive emotional tendencies which exist in others. As a matter of fact, one might well argue that the psychological problems are even greater here than for the layman; after all, the brokers' everyday existence—their economic livelihood—depends on the market itself and on their success therein. Whereas *you* might have a thriving business or a steady job which will continue with or without your smashing success in stocks, those whose income is solely dependent on the market might harbor a conscious or subconscious nervousness about this very area in which they are supposed to be well adjusted.

More important, brokers have huge obstacles to overcome if they are to be the kind of objective, incisive thinkers I have painted as ideal. We know that it is tougher to fight the mob than it is to conform, whether it be manner of living, or dress—or buying stocks. As discussed in chapter 4, it is easier to huddle with others in their buying and selling of stocks than to be contrary—something which is true "in spades" for brokers. *It is far easier, and seems much safer, for brokers to recommend what others are recommending than it is to take an opposing stance.*

Thus, a typical chain of events repeats itself within the investment community in the following pattern:

1. A company or an industry group surfaces in what is stage 1 of our Zigzag chart.

2. News about this company (industry) improves and more people are alerted to it. A limited number of brokers discover the attractiveness of the area.

3. The buying of this group may or may not attract attention (i.e., to chartists of the market), but

the group will ultimately make itself known to a larger and larger number of people through verbal recommendation to clients and associates or written recommendations.

4. Once this group has done its buying, *it will want others to follow.* The desire may be to demonstrate what they expect will be great foresight. Or they may simply want additional buyers to enter the picture and help prove them right immediately (i.e., new buyers might mean higher prices—and it is certainly more pleasant to show profits for your original followers than losses, even if you do not plan to sell the securities at that moment).

5. More and more brokers and investors begin to feel left out. The huddling instinct takes over and the participants satisfy their insecurity through doing what they know others are doing. The rationale is simple: if what others are buying goes up, they participate; and if it goes down, at least the competition is sharing the misfortune.

Furthermore, the followers carry the misconception that there is safety in numbers. As a matter of fact, *they totally misinterpret the supply-demand element of the marketplace* (as explained in chapter 4). They overlook the fact that a host of others recommending purchase have already created exceptional demand—which has produced higher prices. Ideal *selling*—not buying—opportunities exist just when demand has been overly stimulated by this huddling action.

Thus, the most successful investor is the one who recognizes the normal urge to compensate for insecurity, who understands why thinking tends to go to extremes, and how and why inflated demand develops. All this requires a practical comprehension of what it is to be human—which is the prime goal of this book. Understanding this will lead to your becoming an independent shepherd, as opposed to the masses (including many brokers) who act as sheep and bah, bah, bah their way to either a slight shearing, a loss of one year's coat of wool—or even to eventual slaughter!

Bolstering Your Psychological Armament for Beating the Crowd

Understanding how and when to be contrary in the stock market is one thing; having the emotional strength to carry out such a course of action is an entirely different, but obviously crucial, requirement.

By the time you have completed this book, you will understand how there is money to be made following a majority opinion (as in the IBM-type equity), *and* also that there is money to be made from reacting directly opposite to the crowd. In the latter case, you should *not* expect that the masses will suddenly recognize your wisdom the day after you have taken your position. The stock may remain out of favor for some time—until an event such as the release of favorable news awakens the investing public to the values which you had the foresight to anticipate. Waiting for this recognition may try both your patience and your emotions to the point where you are long gone from the stock when prosperity actually develops.

Anyone making imaginative investment decisions has to face this test constantly. A good example occurred for me in 1969. In July of that year I was interviewed at length by *Barron's,* the fine weekly investment publication. When questioned which securities appeared attractive to me, I emphasized Clorox Company—mainly because the stock was under the cloud of enzyme laundry products (which were not to be used in conjunction with a bleach). *Barron's* printed my comments about Clorox and within a few weeks I received countless letters and phone calls from people who disagreed with me. "Bleaches are on their way out," they said in a variety of ways—and with such gusto that I began to wonder if my contrary view was off base.

So I reassessed the situation. In the process, I realized that all the positives of enzymes had been ballyhooed and that no negatives had yet been presented. I reasoned that there might be a questioning of this new additive—or simply that consumers might return to established habits and prefer detergents-plus-bleach again. The fact that the thinking was almost unanimously negative on Clorox was confirmed by the stock's price action. Less than a year before, the price was $33.50, earlier in 1969 it was over $24.00—and then (in July) it was just $16.00–17.00. At that level, incidentally, Clorox stock was selling at only eleven to twelve times earnings which were existing even through the enzyme competition.

So I bolstered my confidence, reminding myself

that it is always darkest before the storm. And I gained courage from what should have been my first reaction to the opinions of others. They were reacting to emotion of the moment and were not leaving room for reasonable doubt. I, instead, recognized that any glint of hope for bleaches would mean higher prices for Clorox stock. The general negativism had taken the stock to levels of unusual value, something which was certain to rule in the end.

The story's end is typical. Within a few months (during which Clorox stock went nowhere and which were filled with doubt whether the thesis was correct), the publicity suddenly turned. Enzymes were first questioned, then criticized—and bleach came back with force. By the end of the year, Clorox stock had risen to $24.00, and twelve months later (December, 1970), it was $34.00. The stock had doubled, during a most difficult period for investors; success emanated from reacting opposite to the crowd and having the strength to hold fast while others were panicking.

In dealing with this type of investment, therefore, it should bolster your psychological armament to follow the reasoning of Leo Model, who says that he may actually be *more* concerned if his sophisticated choices move *up* in price right after he has bought them. He reasons that such quick follow-through makes his original analysis highly suspect. After all, if many others apparently have the same idea as he, then the idea may not be so original after all. As he once wrote to me, "Sometimes the sophisticated investor must look dumb for a while in order to be really smart."

This thought can also reinforce your ability to live with those losses which are associated with timing—as opposed to misjudgment of fundamentals—already discussed in chapter 8.

Expecting Both Clear and Cloudy Weather

This chapter and the previous one emphasize being objective, seeing both sides to any argument, and conditioning your thinking process so that the emotional extremes are tempered. Inherent in this approach is the ability to see through the obvious—and to have the imagination to picture something different.

It's like walking down the street in the middle of a rainstorm, with the temperature a chilly forty degrees. Under such conditions it is most difficult to imagine that tomorrow might bring the sun shining through. Or at least it may be difficult to "feel" the warmth of that sunshine while you are experiencing the cold.

Certainly I do not have to explain that blue skies will eventually prevail—just as it is unnecessary to point out that clear skies will ultimately be followed by clouds. In the stock market, it is wise to remember that the weather is bound to be changeable—and that you should condition yourself for an eventual change of gear. In other words, there is eventually going to be both warmth and cold. Thus, when ideas become so fashionable that they are a way of life, *they should be suspect.*

To conclude, the thinking process which makes the most money for people is one which demands some contrary questioning. This requires more courage; more emotional "steeling"; and it entails greater use of what we will stress in chapter 18—imagination.

An Extra Dividend of New-Era-ism and Objectivity

I can't resist summarizing the thought patterns of this and the previous chapter on what I consider a humorous note. On Februay 1, 1970, Mr. Art Hoppe, whom I consider to be one of the great satirists of our time, wrote a column for his syndicated audience entitled, "The Greatest Generation." With Art's permission, here 'tis:

Once upon a time there was a man named Ben Adam, who, like most members of The Older Generation, had little hair and overwhelming guilt feelings.

He also had a son named Irwin, who, like most members of The Younger Generation, had lots of hair and an overwhelming contempt for anybody over thirty.

"Man, what a mess your generation made of things," Irwin was fond of saying, several times daily. "Because of your bumbling, we face a society that's racist, militaristic, polluted, overpopulated, and terrorized by the hydrogen bomb. Thanks a lot."

"I guess we're about the worst generation that ever lived," Ben Adam would say, nodding guiltily.

"I'm sorry, Irwin." And Irwin would shrug and go off with his friends to smoke pot.

Ben Adam couldn't help feeling that he was in for a bit of divine wrath in return for his sins. And he was therefore somewhat shaken on awakening one night to find an Angel at the foot of his bed writing in a Golden Book.

"I have come, Ben Adam," said the Angel, "to grant you one wish."

"Me?" said Ben Adam with surprise. "Why me?"

"You have been selected by the Heavenly Computer as typical of your generation," said the Angel. "And your generation is to be rewarded for its magnificence."

"There must be some mistake," said Ben Adam with a frown. "We've been awful. We created a racist society . . ."

"Mankind has always been racist," said the Angel gently. "You were the first to admit it and attempt a remedy."

"And we militarized our democracy. Why, when I was a boy, we only had an army of 134,000 men."

"You built an army of four million men in hopes of bringing freedom and democracy to all the world," said the Angel. "Truly, a noble goal."

"Well, maybe," said Ben Adam. "But you can't deny that we polluted the water and the air and scattered garbage far and wide."

"That is so," said the Angel. "But the environment is polluted solely because you constructed the most affluent society the world has ever seen."

"I guess that's right," said Ben Adam. "Yet look

at the Population Explosion. Famine and pestilence threaten mankind."

"Only because your generation cured diseases, increased the food supply, and thereby lengthened man's life span," said the Angel. "A tremendous achievement."

"And we live in the terror of the hydrogen bomb," said Ben Adam gloomily. "What a legacy."

"Only because your generation unlocked the secrets of the atom in its search for wisdom," said the Angel. "What a glorious triumph."

"You really think so?" said Ben Adam, sitting straighter and smiling tentatively.

"Your motives were excellent, your goals ideal, your energies boundless, and your achievements tremendous," said the Angel, reading from the Golden Book. "In the eons of mankind, the names of your generation, Ben Adam, lead all the rest. And therefore, by the authority vested in me, I am empowered to grant you one wish. What shall it be?"

"I wish," said Ben Adam, the heavenly chosen representative of The Older Generation with a sigh, "that you'd have a little talk with Irwin."

Overlooking its leaning towards the Establishment (actually Art's work generally knocks the Old Guard and favors the young 'uns), the essay offers a superb lesson on objectivity and the need for avoiding extremes in one's thinking. Common-stock buyers take heed! Have your enthusiasm but temper it with enough skepticism so that you are objective in your investment approach.

18. Imagination Is—Everything

I have to admit to being of the era in which the song "Imagination" was popular. As a result, each time I hear the word imagination I dwell on some of the verses to the tune, such as:

> Imagination is funny,
> It makes a cloudy day sunny,
> Makes a bee think of honey . . .

Whereas the lyrics have a wonderfully positive tone, a person can make what he wishes out of his own imaginative powers. He can imagine "boogey men" everywhere in his existence, he can imagine himself inferior in all directions, he can look on the sunniest days as being bleak and overcast for a multitude of reasons. In short, he can make mountains out of molehills or the opposite; and he can direct his capacity for happiness or sadness a great deal simply because of his mental approach. Needless to say, one is going to be a heck of a lot happier if the cloudy days are generally viewed through "sunny" eyes. It follows that a person can shape his business and investment destinies through the use of imagination.

While all of this is quite obvious, one might question whether you can teach imagination. Is this not one of those innate traits which we either have or have not—and which we cannot really do much about?

Fortunately, such is *not* the case. Imagination is definitely something about which we can do a great deal. Having been given a brain, we have been provided with a built-in creative mechanism which we can put to work in a variety of ways. If we let it flounder or if we use it incorrectly, it is our *own* doing. It is the ignition switch to success; all we have to do is turn the key.

There are a number of obvious starting points for the person seeking to be imaginative and creative. First of all, you should have *faith*—faith in the fact that your state of mind can be strongly influenced by your own suggestion, faith in your ability to create something unusual simply as a result of your mental effort. Secondly, and I suppose this is really no more than an easier-to-understand definition of faith, you should have *positive* designs and reactions. That is, you must have a *stimulus* to be imaginative and this stimulus is going to come if you are loaded with positive ammunition and an active mind.

Thirdly, you should understand that human beings have a decided tendency to defend habits and long-established thought patterns regardless of whether they still represent what they once did. Thus, a starting point towards the utilization of imagination is to think about changing some of these established patterns.

In addition, imagination should create a feeling of real *excitement.* This does not mean you have to be a dreamer, with strictly ethereal, impractical visions as your daily habit. Imagination can be exciting and down to earth at the same time. Because it is exciting you will experience stimulation, which tends to feed on itself and spur you on to greater and greater things. And because it is practical, your potential for making money in a multitude of directions (yes, including the stock market) is enhanced manyfold.

In order to establish this productive attitude my suggestion is to *make a game of it,* a game which can be played by any number from one (yourself alone) to an infinitely large group. There is no need for dice or a board or any props, and the cost is most reasonable: nothing! The only equipment necessary is your brain.

The object of our game is no more than to train you to think imaginatively, which begins by applying such thought to everything "imaginable." Just as a good actor or athlete brings himself up for each performance, you want to prepare yourself for day-to-day imagination by setting it to work right now. To create the habit, set out to get imaginative kicks from as many areas as possible—even those which might seem bizarre at the moment. Expand whatever vision you possess to take in new vistas and at the same time become an experimenter and a conceptualizer and an inventor and an originator. Let yourself go—and practice in areas such as foods, household products, business, real estate, mechanical aids of all sorts, and products of all sorts.

Let me give you an example. The first of the areas suggested involves foods—something which most of us enjoy, me included. Over the years I have had a great deal of fun experimenting with all types of new food combinations. I suppose that is what the great cooks of the world are doing all the time; my approach has been on a much lower level. To illustrate, I have chewed gum for years. My favorite flavor was cinnamon, but I found that its bite was too strong at times. My second favorite was mint. So what was the obvious experimenter's approach? Why, to take half a piece of cinnamon and half a piece of mint and chew them together. And you know what?—the combination was delicious. Along the way some companions noticed my experimentation and I was amazed at their reaction, which was to laugh at me. They were not scoffing, but they were apparently thinking something like "Gad, what a silly guy—mixing two different types of gum" or "What an eccentric character."

Some people would have been concerned over such reaction. Even though I am basically thin-skinned I frankly found it most amusing. So much so, in fact, that it encouraged me. My reasoning was really quite simple. I knew that my experimenting, silly as it might have been, was an attempt to be creative and imaginative. And that, my friend, is totally constructive.

Actually, their laughter gave me just a little more confidence in my design to be creative and imaginative. While I realize that the misfortunes or inadequacies of others should have little bearing on our own personalities, the mere fact that others smirked at my idiosyncrasy made me feel just a bit more confident in this one area. After all they were the ones who were missing out on the fun and on the prospects which were sure to be forthcoming, and their failure to recognize the potential meant that overall "competition" was minimal.

Incidentally, I used to get an additional giggle when I explained to such observers that I called my combination "Cinnamint." (What else? After all, it was half cinnamon and half mint.)

You gum-lovers know the end of this story. A number of years later, Clark's introduced a flavor which is prominent on the stands today. Its name? You guessed it—Cinnamint.

I may have spent too much time on this insignificant example. Instead I suppose I should have told you how I discovered Polaroid or Xerox or a host of glamour companies which have provided unbelievable gains for their holders, especially those who had the imagination and foresight to recognize them when they began for what they are today. I will touch on this later; for now, be convinced that *imagination is simple, it is fun, it is catching—and it can lead to the big trophies if you foster it.* As mentioned, it's all part of a game; so if you get yourself enough spaces forward at the beginning, your chances of making it all the way to "Go" and $200 are greatly enhanced.

If you can stand it, let the "Cinnamint Kid" give you another ridiculous illustration of imaginative mental conditioning. Shortly after I entered the securities business I had the pleasure of lunching at the Stock Exchange Club in New York City. There I was introduced to a clam juice–tomato juice* cocktail, something which I later found was available at the Stock Exchange Club in San Francisco and in other restaurants. I was enthusiastic over this combination and immediately started experimenting with it at home: a little bit of this, a dash of that—all done with enthusiasm and for the heck of it. Frankly, I thought this combo was a natural and that it should be available through normal food channels. I was too busy to develop anything commercially myself but I well recall the fun I had writing a silly radio-TV jingle and sending this, along with the whole idea, to one of the major food and tomato-juice packers. Not to my surprise, nothing came of it.

Fifteen years later, Mott's hit the market with its "Clamato," which was an instant success. And you know what? I consider *myself* the modern inventor of the commercially available clam-juice and tomato-juice combination!

Now moral victories are not my goal in life, and I have no intention of being an "I told you so" guy. You have to understand that I hold no frustrations about either Cinnamint or Clamato. Quite the con-

*Actually they use catsup instead of tomato juice.

trary, they served to convince me that I am an imaginative and creative person and I know that if I continue to play this game I will succeed in a number of areas. Once again, so long as one is not simply a dreamer (*you have to take action as a result of your inventiveness*), any efforts such as those just described create the right atmosphere and approach for you personally. True, a lot of people may laugh at you, but your chances of ultimately laughing all the way to the bank are greatly improved as a result of such thinking.

The imaginative thinker should expect disagreement from others. Big ideas are seldom recognized for their worth at the beginning. This is important to understand since one secret to stock-market success is in being ahead of the crowd in recognizing unappreciated industries or companies and in recognizing new products which might turn the tables for such entities. This is something on which I have prided myself over the years. Quite honestly most of my greatest stock coups have evolved from a thought pattern not so different from Cinnamint and Clamato. When I imagined color television well before its acceptance and wide usage, I was simply projecting potential enthusiasm; I could feel the animation and excitement of color just as I could taste Cinnamint and Clamato. My latching on to mobile homes while others were still picturing bulky trailers blocking the highway was no more than the enthusiasm for owning a home away from home for $5,000. My discovery of Simplicity Pattern while others considered the business as tangible as cutting paper dolls was, aside from the practicality of saving money through homemade clothing, an extension of the feeling of accomplishment on the part of the sewer. My uncovering Masco and the single-handled faucet was a projection of the value of eliminating two faucets and the experience of having the water first too hot and then too cold. Catching Seven-Up early in its publicly held days involved no more than understanding what consumer acceptance and enthusiasm means to potential sales, earnings, and price-earnings (P-E) multiples. What attracted me to Raychem when people hardly knew what radiation chemistry was, emanated from the exciting thought of wires, cables, and component coverings which could be made to shrink and expand to predetermined "memorized" sizes through the mere application of heat. (The all-important selling signal in Raychem came when this very glamorous product line excited people to the point where the stock no longer represented just a company—it represented a cult, a religion; in short, imagination had created emotions which simply obliterated sound judgment. Needless to say, this is not the kind of imagination I am prescribing.) Naturally, there are thousands of great investment stories which evolved like these and which were no more brilliant than thinking about cinnamon and mint or clam and tomato juice. And which, I should add, generated as much enthusiastic support from outsiders at their inception as did my Cinnamint and Clamato.

Obviously I am urging you to make yourself imagination-conscious—*today!* Whereas we are told that necessity is the mother of invention and adversity is a great teacher, you need not wait for either necessity or adversity to become inventive, imaginative, and creative. Aside from the fact that this will put more spring in your step and in your mind (imagination creates energy), and that your happiness quotient will expand sharply, your investment success will get the shot-in-the-arm it deserves. You see, *imagination negates prejudices and encourages openmindedness*—an ideal combination for productive stock portfolios. It is always revealing to compare the stock list of a person who is utilizing imagination with that of the uncreative individual. I can tell at a glance whether the mental attitude is progressive or not and, most important, the dollar results will reflect it. Indeed, imagination can, and should, be utilized to make your investing days sunny. The sooner you commence developing such great habits, the better your performance will be and the sooner your investment goals will be achieved.

The Importance of Becoming "Expectational"

One very practical part of applying imagination to stock investing is the understanding of *expectation* as a determinant of market prices. Whereas *value*—in the form of asset values or earning power—will ultimately determine the worth of securities, there is no denying that stocks sell on the basis of what people *think* they are worth. Why else do two companies possessing similar earnings per share, and growing at approximately the same rate, sell at vastly different prices? Why else do industries or companies whose characteristics do not change substantially swing from low to high levels and then back again? Why else do people pay astronomical figures for the flimsiest of outfits and yet have the tendency to overlook completely some stocks which possess unbelievable values? As Chief Justice Oliver Wendell Holmes observed so rightly over eighty years ago, "All values are anticipations of the future."

Yes, it is the *opinion* of things, much of which is based on limited study or thought, which can gild the lily—or the reverse. Here, of course, is where the emotional and psychological aspects which we have been discussing really come to bear. To succeed to the fullest in the stock market, it is imperative to understand this and to master as well as possible the art of *proper expectation.*

There is some validity to the thesis that stock prices are always the product of hope, greed, or fear—all three of which are human expectations. In the case of hope, it is the expectation that things will get better. In the case of greed, it is the expectation that they will get better—and better—and better. And in the event of fear, it is simply the expectation of the worst.

The most successful investors are those *who comprehend the potentials from these expectational forces.* By anticipating crowd reactions, they are better judges of general market behavior and of individual stock prices. In addition, by isolating the same human tendencies in themselves, they have better control of themselves and form good judgment. Stated more simply, they control their own destinies more efficiently, rather than becoming victims of their emotions and those of others.

The secret to proper expectation in the stock market, therefore, is a blending of imagination and enthusiasm—with a governor on both so that rational thought constantly prevails. Part of this is the expectation of higher profits from any company considered for investment. Part of it has to do with the sort of conceptualizing which was behind the color TV, Simplicity Pattern, Masco, Seven-Up, and other successes illustrated on pages 183–84. And part of it entails a guesstimate of the kind of reasonable enthusiasm which might be expected from others in *their* evaluation of the securities. Thus, it is once again an understanding of the *expectational* elements which will dictate the results.

Certainly this emphasis relegates scientific procedures to the back seat—but then this is what *Psycho-Cybernetics and the Stock Market* is all about. Knowing how and when to utilize the power of imagination and understanding when others have become carried away is that fine touch—that all-important intuitive element—which separates the relatively few successful men from the mass of floundering boys in the Money Game.

Let me here caution all imagination-users from a concept which became standard procedure in those ridiculous stock-market days of 1967–68. At that time, many people made money from what I call the "Greater Fool" principle. Many took to buying stocks almost solely on the basis that others' stupidity (uncontrolled emotions would be a kinder term) would raise the prices still further. As in the famous tulip mania in Holland in the seventeenth century, the fact that bulbs were selling far beyond their intrinsic value was insignificant relative to the widespread thought that others' emotions would drive them to buy impulsively. That is what I was referring to above when I insisted that a governor is needed to control both imagination and enthusiasm.

It is one thing to anticipate a reasonable degree of enthusiasm from others; it is another to expect them to exhibit utter stupidity and to hinge your success on such idiocy. Furthermore, our quest for investing serenity is certainly endangered by following such a Greater Fool ploy.

Thus, it is imperative to distinguish proper imagination and thought from uncontrolled imagination. The stock market of 1970 is littered with the skeletons of those who could not make this distinction—and markets of the future will likely reflect the same phenomenon.

19. On How And When To Drag Down Profits

There is an ancient Wall Street adage which states: "A bull can make money in stocks; a bear can make money in stocks; but a *hog* never can."

Inherent in this axiom is advice that stocks are bought *to be sold,* which means that investors should not cling too long to their holdings and that when they are presented with a good profit they ought to take it and run.

Whereas this dictum appears sound, the whole thing breaks down because of a necessary definition of what a "good profit" really is. Or, said in the language of the adage, at what point does a person become a hog? When he has made 50 percent on his money, 100 percent, 300 percent, or what?

Certainly no one figure constitutes the answer, just as no general answer satisfies the question. This hardly means, however, that we should avoid the problem and not seek out as precise a solution as possible—which is just what I intend to do.

Perhaps an ideal starting point is to relate stock investing to the advice of an old-fashioned father who instructed his son that "There are gals who are for fooling around, and there are those who are for marrying." Relating this to equities, if we can only differentiate between those which are best purchased for temporary thrills and those which are best lived with, *we have at least substantially narrowed down the problem.*

As would be expected, the psychological approach to these two investment categories differs widely. The to-be-lived-with group, which will be emphasized in the next chapter, requires a calm and patient attitude and a concerted effort to stick around for the serenity of old age. The other category, which contains the great majority of stocks, demands a *programmed nervousness*—no, let's call it programmed *questioning*—in order that we simultaneously maximize our gains and not become hogs.

Directing ourselves to this latter group, we will be mentally well prepared if we understand at the very outset that:

1. We must eventually make *two* decisions, that of buying the stock in mind and that of eventually selling it. We must remind ourselves constantly that

the selling *will* be necessary and that the security is not to accompany us to the grave.

2. The ideal selling opportunity is going to be when others form together in a crowd, which will hike market prices to typical fadlike, inflated levels.

3. We should objectively appraise the stock through a combination of our Industry Strength Guide, an all-important understanding of business cycles, and most particularly how cycles occur within cycles, as per the Zigzag chart in chapter 17. We should base specific buy-and-sell decisions according to an assessment of position within such cycles.

Thus, it is a matter of assessing the true characteristics of an industry or a company; never losing sight of this position; telling yourself that you are going to be ahead of the crowd and act opposite to it when gloom and enthusiasm prevail; and to act when such extremes occur in the market or when it appears as if cyclical tendencies are going to take over.

Do not misunderstand! I am *not* suggesting that the buying and selling of securities can be made into a true science and that any chart, formula or guide can supply the answers. What I am saying is that a disciplined approach involving basic fundamentals along with controlled emotions can raise your batting average enormously.

Maximizing returns from some of the coups described in the last chapter emanated from this kind of simple discipline. For example, Zenith was obviously part of the Radio-TV group shown in our Industry Strength Guide as cyclical (directly sensitive to the overall economy) and its strength within the category was only in the number 3 category (where 4 is low). What this meant was: condition yourself to the idea of selling it; do not get so enamored with its prospects, regardless of your enthusiasm for a color revolution, that you plan to live with it forever. In this case, the selling tip-off came from the crowd reaction, which suddenly lifted the group from its earlier low P-E multiples to those of glamour proportions. *Actually, any and all of the industries in cyclical categories I or II will be best sold when they gain any semblance of popularity in the market.* Back to Zenith, the 1961 market saw a recognition of the whole Radio-TV group by the investment community. High P-E multiples, as mentioned, were one sign of overenthusiasm. Equally important were some intangibles which were really responsible for the high market prices existing at the time. These intangibles were, and are, as good a guide to knowing when to drag down profits as anything mathematical. They included:

1. The Radio-TV industry suddenly became the subject of a host of research reports by brokers and investment services;

2. Typical reaction—and as good a sign as any that uncontrolled, naïve buyers have now hopped on the bandwagon—included a market play in the industry's weak sisters. In 1961, for example, Admiral and Emerson and other previously unsuccessful companies suddenly became darlings of Wall Street. The coup de grâce occurred when National Video, a company which did nothing but supply tubes to (mainly) one set manufacturer, also became a market favorite.

(National Video eventually declared bankruptcy, in 1969.)

3. Portfolios of mutual funds and other institutional investors suddenly showed large holdings in this industry.

Said another way, investors' emotions reached such a wave of enthusiasm that the true spots of the leopard were forgotten.

Mobile-home stocks provided similar ideal grab-your-profits circumstances in 1969. Interesting as the future might have appeared, the group had to be recognized as cyclical—although in this case such sensitivity was related not so much to the general economy as to overall demand for housing and the availability of money for time purchases of the products. Thus, the word "cyclical" alone was the warning buzzer to the stock buyer; and the fact that the industry was not even rated as the strongest in the grouping constituted an additional bit of programmed questioning.

The three glaring signs of impending disaster listed in the Zenith example had now reared their ugly heads. Brokers and investment services were on the mobile-home bandwagon; the "dogs" of the industry were having their play; and the large investors couldn't resist the temptation to showcase their portfolios by inclusion of mobile-home equities, previously not represented.

In addition, the group was showing the kind of business behavior discussed in chapter 17's zigzag. All one had to do was to read the *Wall Street Journal* to know that the apparent attractiveness of the business was leading to new entries and enlarged capacity. What with some of the biggest names in industry (e.g., Boise Cascade) now in the swim, the supply side of the all-important supply-demand equation was obviously in for a large increase.

Anyone who understood business' 1-to-6 typical pattern (as shown on page 166) realized that conditions were changing in the industry. And understanding how the masses normally react to such conditions (the bottom part of the Zigzag chart) converted the warning buzzer of his first impressions into an absolute siren.

It is interesting to look at the Industry Strength Guide and see that *each and every group within cyclical categories I and II is one which should have been liquidated at some time in the past in order to achieve the ultimate in capital appreciation.* And while you may disagree with strength ratings within the broad groupings, I find it hard to believe that future investments in these industries will not require the same flexibility.

But How About the Noncyclicals?

I said that those stocks of the marrying kind would be covered in chapter 21. Naturally not all of the noncyclicals qualify for this relaxed attitude. As a matter of fact, most of the industries in category III require an approach approximating that appropriate to I and II (see pages 57–58). The questions to pose are the very ones listed above, with the main difference being that the urgency is generally not quite so great. Still, a disciplined questioning is in order, which we will complete in a moment.

Conclusions

Admitting again that there is no one solution to the problem of when to sell securities, the kind of programmed questioning emphasized gives you a decided advantage over your competition in the stock market. Even though buying and selling based on general market conditions has been omitted, your ability to discipline yourself in the manner described is going to give you a decided emotional advantage over the great bulk of participants. Referring to the adage mentioned at the outset of this chapter, you now understand that the hog in the stock market is the one who gets so caught up in his emotions that he cannot differentiate between really solid stocks and those with an attractive facade. Skin-deep beauty alone is hardly the basis for the ultimate in relationships—in people and stocks. You now possess the upper hand in that you recognize this, have the potential for control over your investing emotions, and actually comprehend the approach to dragging down profits. You have learned to be the "correctly parental" investor suggested in chapter 4.

20. I *Can* Stand Prosperity

Investing in the stock market requires *change of pace* in that there are times when you have to "think sell" and times when you want to be extra patient. The problem lies in knowing when to be which.

Having already discussed that part of the stock market which demands extra flexibility and concentration on dragging down profits, let's now move to those which require a somewhat detached and patient attitude. Don't worry, this will not be just another "Patience is a virtue" sermon. Indeed, patience is a virtue, but it can also be mistaken for out-and-out *stubbornness, indecision, laziness, or inertia.*

One important trait of an astute investor is the ability to distinguish patience from these other restrictive characteristics—something which the Industry Strength and Zigzag guides can accomplish.

For example, one of the attractive-*appearing* industries in the market in the mid-1960s was that of synthetic fibers; many, many portfolio managers were betting heavily on the group's prospects through ownership of Du Pont, Monsanto, and others. Price-earnings ratios were already better than twenty, but these managers looked to a combination of higher profits and possibly some upward revision of the P-E multiple to bring them a decent return from these stocks.

Frankly, the prospects looked just the opposite to me, based solely on what Industry Strength and zigzag analysis indicated. For one thing, the chemicals were then (as today) in the cyclical category, although their strength was such that they were best classified as *semi*cyclical. Still, the question remained whether a semicyclical group deserved P-Es of over twenty. I felt they did not, mainly because no other in their category commanded anywhere near such an evaluation. Most important, I was conscious of zigzags and the fact was that the industry had very large capacity coming on-stream over the next few years. Actually, the "trap" of becoming enthusiastic just when everyone else was—which was just when competition was heightening—had been set. Every few weeks the *Wall Street Journal* would carry a news item indicating the glorious expansion plans of one company or another, which to most people spelled reason for optimism. Brokers reacted accordingly, with glowing reports on the prospects for the industry. And the huddling instinct discussed in chapter 4 merely fostered the already developed enthusiasm.

The results may have seemed startling to some, what with stocks such as Du Pont and Monsanto dropping to half their values from that time to 1969—at the very time other stocks were faring very well. As I hope you now realize, however, these events were totally typical of business and the stock market.

As should also be apparent, the tip-off to the correct advice came from our disciplines. Categorizing industries according to their cyclical nature combined with a basic understanding of how business behaves was far more important than any detailed knowledge a person might have had about chemicals. As a matter of fact, I couldn't even pronounce half the technical terms which the chemical analysts and portfolio managers counted on for exciting growth. In a way, this was an excellent example of how *practical* analysis and approach is superior to the theoretical.

Airline stocks over the last three or four years mirror the same picture. Institutions and the public fell in love with what was a definite cyclical industry with added detriments of high labor costs and governmental regulation. Once again the key was found in understanding zigzags. Figures on airline capacity related to normal demand came up highly negative and this led to a deterioration of profits. Like the chemicals, market action through 1969 was disastrous.

In the noncyclical category, the computer software stocks went through a feast-and-famine experience in which the famine should have been apparent to everyone. Whereas there was no doubt that the 1970s would bring with them tremendous demands for software capability, the business attracted so many new entries that a zigzag was really a lead-pipe cinch. Software constituted a "people" business with great ease of entry. In 1968 and 1969, hardly a week went by that I didn't hear of a new, small group (usually consisting of several former IBM "geniuses") going into business. Despite this market flooding, investors went goofy over the glamour attached to the industry and hiked the prices of these equities to typical fad proportions. Before long, the figures began to show (the operating losses, that is) and of course the group came full tilt: exuberance and enthusiasm swung to outright pessimism, as zigzag triumphed again!

I could cite countless examples similar to these—examples of how investors could not distinguish fact from fiction. While hindsight is always 20–20, the industry strengths and zigzags most often were waving the flags of warning.

When Then Patience?

The starting point, therefore, for the use of patience is proper selection. Granted this, patience is a great virtue; without it, it tends to be stubbornness or laziness.

Those fields which command the high-strength ratings in the noncyclical category of our Industry Strength Guide constitute one criterion for good selection. Remember, however, that industry attractiveness never remains static. Many of the weaker industries of today were yesterday's growth stocks; and certain of the stable and cyclical groups of today may emerge as something more glamorous in the future. Still, if the guide is at all accurate, most of the 1 rated fields in category III represent investments in which the ability to hold fast should prove to be most rewarding. So here we come to the title of this chapter, which relates to the ability to stand prosperity.

That there is difficulty in very good fortune may surprise you. Proof, however, lies in the stockholder records of companies such as IBM, Xerox, Avon, and the like, which are absolutely littered with the "bodies" of former shareholders who couldn't make it through for the big payoff. Strange as it may seem, many people become as nervous with sizable gains as they do with losses; and to get them to "guts it out" and remain undisturbed long enough to wait for the tripling, quadrupling, quintupling, and higher potential for their dollars is surely one of the tougher things to accomplish.

Why, you might ask, are some investors so "antsy" with their profits and possibly (even at the same moment) relatively undisturbed by losses? This is something I talked about in *The Common Sense Way to Stock Market Profits*, wherein I ascribed the phenomenon to:

1. The person able to live with a loss may do so because he is the procrastinator type who shuts his eyes to reality or who wrongly thinks "I don't have a loss until I actually sell the security."

2. The Wall Street adage that "No one ever went broke taking a profit" is firmly inbued in the minds of investors and stockbrokers alike; this, plus the adage already alluded to about hogs in the stock market, tends to make many too anxious to sell.

3. A psychological moment seems to arrive when one has doubled one's money. In other words, there is a natural tendency to unload once a dollar has been turned into two.

4. Brokers themselves (many at least) are too commission-conscious and tend to prod clients into moving before they really should.

5. Many people fear kicking themselves in the pants (see chapter 11). Thus, the thought of having a stock go from twenty dollars to forty dollars—and then back to twenty dollars—contains the greatest possibilities for remorse and for the potential pants-kicking reaction.

6. Not enough people learn to have confidence and to relax sufficiently with the right stocks.

7. Investors have no conception of the wisdom of accumulating just a few (that is all that is generally necessary) stocks which do famously in one's lifetime; thus, $5,000 or $10,000 held in a few stocks which go up five, ten, or more times amounts to "many marbles."

All these reasons bear on the person who cannot stand prosperity. Your understanding them should help to eliminate any such tendency.

A few other elements are necessary if we are to achieve the ultimate and learn to live with those superprosperous stocks. A starting point involves having confidence in a system like that provided by our two guides. The Industry Strength Guide, subjective though it be, is the product of strong historical evidence, which in turn is a product of the basic characteristics of the industries listed. Combining this with a practical look at business does give you a discipline which others frankly lack.

A second element of understanding involves a willingness to go along with superior management and to recognize that these people may be smarter than stock analysts, brokers, or even *ourselves.* It never ceases to amaze me how really good, imaginative managements tend to surprise you *on the upside.* Their ability to make new moves can overcome all the superanalytical efforts at determining exactly what P-E multiple is appropriate at any given moment. When I think back, for example, on companies such as Bristol-Myers, Johnson & Johnson, IBM, Simplicity Pattern, Masco, Pinkerton's, Seven-Up, Xerox Polaroid, and many others which have proved to be big winners for my clients, I am thankful for the humility to admit that the people running these outfits were damned smart and that confidence in them was more important than trying to pinpoint precise buy and sell levels. In those cases, the reported earnings which resulted far exceeded my original expectations and had I been itchy to pull the trigger and unload early, my people would have missed the five, ten, and even forty times their money multiplied.

This brings up the question of how to rate management. In other words, how does the layman distinguish between those companies which have average leadership and those with people who are really superior and which therefore qualify for extended duration of ownership. Hopefully, someone in a research capacity will help to quantify this for you, but then this runs the risk of sheeplike behavior for which the investment community is noted. Aside from someone's subjective view, one should start with a company's past record; this may not exactly indicate the future, but it should offer a strong clue as to whether the right decisions have been made. In addition, you can form good judgment from an assessment of a company's record of introducing successful new products; the ability to market these items; recent trends of profit margins (pretax profits as a percentage of sales); general corporate moves such as diversification which "fits" as opposed to random conglomeration; reliability of prior forecasts (which is an indication of management's grasp of its own business and its budgeting abilities). Whereas I am the first to admit that management assessment is an intangible, correct rating in a broad sense is extremely valuable. Certainly the skills of companies such as those listed above are so obvious that you need little outside help. And your decision to hold on to the stock should be equally apparent.

A third factor in conditioning yourself to patience is to recognize that the general stock market is very difficult to predict. This is not to say that you should close your eyes to trends, but the person who is jumpy because of his obsession with daily and weekly action has a patience hurdle to overcome. For the sake of this discussion, do not lose sight of the fact that many individual stocks will do well through pretty dismal markets; and the stocks which are usually affected least by declines are the very ones emphasized here—where profits stand to expand sharply even through difficult economic environments.

To prove the wisdom of patience with the right investments, I compiled a list of the most representative companies in seven industry groups which qualified in strength characteristic 1 of category III of the Industry Strength Guide. This included the following industries: computer and office equipment, cosmetics, drugs (proprietary), hospital supply, photography, services, and soft drinks. The companies chosen were IBM, Xerox; Avon, Chesebrough-Pond's, Max Factor, and Revlon; American Home Products, Bristol-Myers, Miles Labs, Plough, Sterling, and Warner-Lambert; American Hospital, Baxter Labs, and Johnson & Johnson; Eastman Kodak and Polaroid; American Express, Dun & Bradstreet, A. C. Nielsen, and Pinkerton's; and Coca-Cola, Dr. Pepper, and Pepsico.

Investment results in these firms over the past five to ten years ranged from startling to very worthwhile. Interestingly, while most of the stocks benefited from a higher rating by the investment community over the period, almost all the companies would have brought decent appreciation to their owners based solely on growth in per-share earnings.

Once again, there is no guarantee that the future will parallel the past but every indication points to still-attractive prospects over at least the next few years.

As will be explained in the next chapter, a well-structured portfolio will contain a foundation of industries and companies such as these, and they will be balanced with not-so-well-regarded companies.

Lastly, it is probably wise to repeat that the wisdom of holding certain stocks is in no way a plug for laziness, indecision, stubbornness, or inertia. Prediction through selection is still required. And action, which may be no more than reassessment to determine whether the industry position still holds true, is still necessary.

Conclusions

Back to the Psycho-Cybernetic thesis, your investment self-image should be improved considerably from:

a. Knowing that you possess a discipline which others lack;

b. Realizing that such discipline has both scientific and practical elements to it; and

c. Understanding which areas require programmed questioning and which demand extra patience.

The result should be an ability to enjoy* prosperity—an attitude which should enhance your wealth handsomely over the years.

*"Enjoy" is a better word than "stand," which carries a connotation of difficulty with it.

21. I Think I Can, I Think I Can

When my children were at the ages where they fit on my lap and where they listened intently to story-telling, there were certain tales which delighted me as much as them—like Dr. Seuss and Winnie the Pooh. And like a great little story entitled "I Think I Can," which relates the adventure of a tiny choochoo train engine which was thought by its owners to have become obsolete because of its size. The bright and shining big locomotives had entered the yard and it was these monsters—not the little choochoo—that the railroad was counting on for heavy duty.

As the story goes, a big job came to the railroad to haul some goods over difficult terrain and most particularly over one big hill which loomed as the major obstacle to reaching the destination.

As you might already guess, the big locomotives were called upon to do the job and, big as they were, they simply couldn't get themselves over this one tough mountain. As a matter of fact, they shuddered and griped at the very thought. All the while, the poor little choochoo sat in the yard unwanted, unpopular, uneverything.

To shorten the story, all the locomotives failed and in final desperation the task was finally given to our forgotten little soul. When asked (choochoos *do* talk, you know) whether the hill could be climbed, our little hero did not accept defeat before the effort was even made; the reply instead was "I think I can."

The rest of the tale is obvious. They hooked the load to the little choochoo and off he went to tackle the impossible. His attitude along the way, however, was positive and when he reached the mountain he put every last effort into the goal in mind. With each puff of the engine he repeated "I think I can," with the "think" taking the timing of the puff itself. Thus, starting with a slower pace he puffed "I——*think*——I can" and then faster "I—*think*—I can" and then faster "I *think* I can." I *think* I can, I *think* I can, I *think* I can. Until, by golly, he was up and over the obstacle—and a hero in the eyes of all.

I will never forget the thrill and happiness of my kids as they puffed with me through the story. More important, the lesson involved was, I thought, excellent. And though it might seem silly, there is an analogy here having to do with investors. In short, it is essential to think you can achieve success in stocks and once you are convinced that you can, your very chances of making it over the hill are increased greatly (recall our discussion on luck and making your own breaks). Thus, I imagine you started this book with a "I think I can" approach—which has, I hope, now changed to "I *know* I can."

Part of this confidence should emanate from the simple understanding of how little money you have to put away on a regular basis to accumulate large sums (chapter 10), and part of it should be derived from the knowledge that you now possess a sound philosophy and discipline to guide your thoughts. Most important, you have explored the all-important psychological elements and you are putting your subconscious to work *for* you, rather than against you. An additional aid is to make sure you are a goal-oriented individual. Realistic goals, properly approached, are usually achieved. If, for example, your usual investment unit is $5,000, set objectives for the future in the stocks you purchase. *Differentiate between those which are going to require flexibility and those which are "stickaways,"* and do not be afraid to project some of these units growing to $15,000, $20,000, or more. You will want to reassess your holdings constantly and be flexible where it is required, but you should be able to enjoy prosperity, too. The mere confidence from knowing that $5,000 of a Xerox might in five years constitute a $10,000 or $15,000 plum for you will do wonders to relax you and build your confidence.

Earlier I alluded to my belief that a person can earn 10 to 15 percent per year on his money through stocks. While selection of individual issues is naturally going to be the key to such performance, the mere *structuring* of a portfolio correctly can go a long way towards the achievement itself. To illustrate, I divide an average portfolio into five basic segments, as follows:

1. Thirty-five percent into *recognized growth* companies—those which are admittedly selling at multiples that reflect their stature but which are growing at 10 to 15 percent annual rates and which carry a large confidence factor. All these stocks represent the top strength of the noncyclical category of our Industry Strength Guide and few of them should expect zigzag earnings results. Assuming P-E multiples remain fairly static in the future, the 10 to 15 percent annual growth (plus 1 to 2 percent average annual yields) should return 10 to 15 percent per year for their owners over the years. This figure is nothing startling, but the confidence factor is high and, as mentioned in chapter 20, the superb managements in question may well surprise you on the upside. Companies which have constituted this "foundation" category for me in the past have been IBM, Xerox, Johnson & Johnson, Avon, and Coca-Cola (occasionally 3M, Eastman Kodak, and Merck, too).
2. Around 25 percent in *high-quality* companies which are in attractive areas, but which

do *not* seem to be *fully recognized* by the investment community. Most would also be in the strong positions in the noncyclical segments of our Industry Strength Guide, but some would be fine companies which might be in stages 1, 4, or 5 of our business zigzag. Growth rates of these companies should equal or exceed 15 percent annually and since I would be looking for some multiple revision upward, a goal of 20 to 25 percent per year would be realistic (yields would be small). Companies which have been good illustrations of this grouping for me have been Simplicity Pattern, Seven-Up, Utah Construction, and Pinkerton's.

3. Approximately 15 percent in *conservative,* low-volatility situations, where growth is 8 to 10 percent, where P-E multiples are low and where yields are decent. The combination of 8 percent growth plus 5 percent yield places potential return in the 10 to 15 percent per annum category.
4. Around 10 percent in *cyclical* situations which are now in the doghouse and which might double or triple over a few years. Thus, annual return goals should be in the 25 to 50 percent area. (Margin of error for each of these groups will be discussed in a moment.)
5. Approximately 15 percent in so-called *special situations.* These might be fast-growth companies, like Levitz or like Raychem once was, where you are willing to pay a premium multiple; or, most probably, in unseasoned situa-

tions which you can envision becoming more popular in the near future. In the latter, you are looking for both earnings improvement and multiple revision upwards and this double-barreled effect should bring about large gains. Selection of stocks in this category should only be made when they hold potential for appreciation of 50 percent per year; the margin of error is obviously going to be larger and the hope is that such errors will still allow for overall return of at least 25 percent annually.

Needless to say, the above is broad in design and it hardly applies to everyone. Some investors might have half their portfolio in the chancier special-situation category—and some might have little or nothing here. The answer lies in one's financial backing and position, as well as with personality and temperament. In addition, the popularity of each grouping—as well as the condition of the general economy—will alter from time to time the percentages in each of the five categories represented.

Once again, the structure may seem useless without the all-important proper selection process. Thus, it is all meaningless if each stock within each category is so bad that it never achieves anything close to the goals in mind. I hope that what has preceded will improve selection for you and that this, plus the structure, will place you in a position of receiving a good rate of return on your dollars *without extreme risk.*

Naturally there is a margin of error involved in every stock analysis. Relating this error to each group, the usefulness of the structure perhaps becomes more apparent. Here, for example, is how a $100,000 portfolio might work out, utilizing the percentages mentioned and allowing for "reasonable losses."

Category	Approx. % of List	Annual Return Expected, %	Reasonable Margin of Error, %	Net Return After Error, %	Dollars Returned After Error
Recognized Growth	35	10–15	20	8 –12	$ 2,800–$ 4,200
Semi-recognized Growth	25	20–25	30	14 –17½	3,500– 4,400
Conservative	15	10–15	15	8½–12½	1,200– 1,800
Cyclical	10	25–50	50	12½–25	1,200– 2,500
Special Situation	15	50	50	25	3,700– 3,700
Total	100				$12,400– 16,600

What this is meant to show is that *you get what you pay for* and that your investment portfolio should allow for this risk versus return tradeoff; for example, those areas which offer the lower annual returns (i.e., recognized growth and conservative) also carry the lowest margin of error, but their anticipated return *after error* is likewise well below that of the others.

What this also indicates is that annual returns of 12 to 16 percent are not unreasonable, understanding of course that they might be above or below this range depending on how you weight your list by categories. Needless to say, the country's overall economic climate will have a great deal to do with what these figures might be. In a healthy atmosphere, the figures are very much doable; but if the nation continues to suffer from inflation and profit-squeeze problems, something considerably below might be the best one can do.

Despite all the variables, there is real strength in a structured approach such as the one suggested. Goodness knows many billions of dollars—and how much nervousness—would have been saved in 1969 and 1970 had people utilized it. Instead, too many got wrapped up in a total-growth concept and poured large portions of their assets into the special-situation category—which carried significant error possibilities with it. The economic climate would not support a large success quotient; and the market had exaggerated the demand side of the equation to the point where the error figure was more like 90 percent, not 50 percent, all of which led to disastrous results.

Thus, the discipline of structuring your investments forces you to greater realism. It places risk in its proper perspective and provides some expectation of what reasonable rewards might be.

Conclusions

The combination of goals and the disciplines plus the emotional ammunition given you, which certainly separate you from those other go-nowhere locomotives, should change any doubts to "I think I can." No—come to think of it, the "I think I can" is really "I *know* I can."

Interruptions are, of course, inevitable as markets have their problems and as the selection process carries errors with it. Still, using the thought pattern just described will minimize huffing and puffing and maximize chances for moving towards financial security and rewards over time. You may not literally zoom to riches, but your chances of actually achieving success—and being relaxed and happy in the process—are greatly enhanced as a result of the general approach.

22. Win It For The Gipper

Remember the dramatic story of the famous Notre Dame gridiron star George Gipp, whose premature death ultimately became the genesis of another great Knute Rockne tale? As a consequence of Gipp's ill fate and his request that "Some day, Rock, when the going is real tough, ask the boys to beat Army for me," Rockne inspired the 1928 Fighting Irish to the point where they emerged from the locker room with blood in their eyes to upset a highly favored Army eleven. Win it for the Gipper they did, mainly because of mental conditioning and because their goal became something more than a game of football.

I hope this book has created a Knute Rockne spirit and attitude for you in your chosen game of investing dollars. Whether your incentive is for you alone or for mom or for those appreciative little rascals who hopefully will busy themselves with more than picking daisies as a result of your wealth, the building blocks should now be in place. Your arsenal combines the psychological and emotional aspects of investing (heretofore little explored) with sound and imaginative investment thinking. As a result, you stand to be a spontaneous, intuitive *winner.*

In addition, your reading has prepared you for the ultimate: *investment happiness.* In our very first chapter I stated that it is senseless to work for a bundle of dollars and to become a bundle of nerves in the process. Thus:

IH does *not* $= BB + N$,

where IH is Investment Happiness, BB is Bundle of Bucks (dollars), and N is Nervousness.

IH does, however, $= SB + EA$,

where SB is Sufficient Bucks, and EA is Emotional Adjustments.

Thus, there is a definite continuity of thought. It is essential to have the psychological and emotional blocks in place in order to maximize investment results. And those very dollars are truly satisfying only when they are accompanied by the same psychological and emotional adjustments. My approach has been to enable you to eat well and sleep well, at the same time.

Certainly your understanding of the preceding

chapters should have reduced anxieties and tensions in a realistic way. In accomplishing this, let there be no misconception about what a well-adjusted investor is. Or what he is *not*.

He is *not* Superman. He is the Happy Medium between No Confidence and Overconfidence. He is neither the person who believes he is a born loser nor the gunslinger of 1967–69, who possessed no humility and who thought he had the answers to everything. Ego is in place, subordinated to *judgment*.

The tack here, of course, has been to emphasize the psychological aspects, both because they are so crucial and because the area has generally been neglected up to now. While I offered derivations of certain investment hangups, this was not my major concentration. I am the first to admit that my psychiatry is amateurish. I lay no claim to anything medical. All I do claim is that what I have observed over the years is practical, at least insofar as making money is concerned.

My use of Psycho-Cybernetics differs from its normal design. Because, as explained, self-image is but a small part of success in a pursuit such as stock investing. In other words, there is no sense in your affirming to yourself that you are an astute investor until you truly are. Furthermore, advice which hinges on the suggestion to come up smiling *when you are still failing* is not very reasonable.

Despite this, there definitely is a need for a form of Psycho-Cybernetics once it has been adapted to the new kinds of input and the facts and approaches specific to the field of stock-market investing. The need for proper feedback to your brain is, of course, the key—something which should already be causing you to react correctly on a more consistent basis. Actually, your reading should have created the "closed loop" which is found in all cybernetic processes. This feedback pattern is the self-regulator which establishes you as the Complete Investor you obviously have sought to be.

I have used the word "intuition" a number of times throughout the book, and held out the goal of becoming an intutitive investor. Actually, intuition is what *Psycho-Cybernetics and the Stock Market* is all about—because a spontaneous reaction based on the right original inputs is going to lead to performance which will enhance your self-image, your happiness, and your pocketbook. The word "cybernetics" comes from the Greek, meaning "helmsman," and it is the right kind of steering which your mind has now absorbed which will enable you to guide your financial ship safe and sound into port.

Essential to this achievement, of course, is the willingness to *continue* to put your mind to work in a positive way. Some people just automatically think this way. Others have to make a concerted effort to practice it. This simply means that you should assess your own habits and your need for self-discipline and be sure that you don't let your learning cease now. The prospects are great in a variety of ways.

Some even use this mental programming to enhance their physical prowess. For example, Mike Garrett, the former University of Southern California halfback who made it big with the 1969 world champions of professional football, the Kansas City Chiefs, and Wes Parker, the Los Angeles Dodgers first baseman. In January, 1970, a syndicated article appeared in the nation's newspapers entitled "Garrett's Mind Rules His Body," which singled out Psycho-Cybernetics as Mike's weapon "to combat the deep depression which threatened his career." Garrett, so the article stated, understood that the mind "is simply a computer and you can make it do what you want it to. And that control of your mind will give you control of your body."

"After a while," said Mike, "you train your mind like a computer—put the ideas in, digest it, and the body acts accordingly." As a result, Garrett went from a poor year in 1968 to a banner performance in 1969.

Wes Parker went through the same kind of "improve myself" thinking. Once labeled as strictly good-field, no-hit, he was introduced to Psycho-Cybernetics in 1968 and experienced exceptional results in 1969. "I like to think," he says, "that I am a good example of what Psycho-Cybernetics can do. I believe in it completely. Self-confidence is the most important thing if you're a ballplayer or a banker. The mental approach is the key to happiness and success."

Back to the all-important subject of *you,* your potential for improvement is just as pertinent as it was with Garrett and Parker. While their goals may be to pile up yardage or garner more base hits, yours can range all the way from becoming a happier person or a more understanding individual to being a truly successful investor who can accumulate a great deal of money in your lifetime (and not become tense in the process).

The starting point is the willingness to listen and the desire to be more and more of a doer. Contrary to the song from *Snow White and the Seven Dwarfs* about "Wishing (Will Make it So)," you need to take constructive action through:

1. Reviewing the data presented, particularly those which "ring a bell" relative to your own investment makeup; and

2. Substituting constructive inputs for those which were either lacking or which were inhibiting you in your investing process.

Realizing that garbage in creates garbage out, your own GIGO should now become Goodies In bring Goodies Out. Here, for example, is a review of the more significant thoughts which have been presented and which constitute a basis for proper investment attitude.

1. There is an uncomplicated, logical approach to stock investing.

2. By knowing yourself and understanding others, you have a decided competitive advantage in the market.

3. There is a way to invest in stocks and be reasonably relaxed in the process.

4. It is essential to have serenity along with your quest for economic achievement; as a matter of fact, this serenity is an integral part of this achievement.

5. Risk is not associated solely with offensive strategy. Indeed, the least risk may well come from a well-planned offense.

6. Some losses are inevitable, but a reduction of related anxieties and an understanding of how losses tend to be exaggerated can place them in their proper perspective.

7. There is a way of working with others who are closely involved with your investment decisions (e.g., you can develop proper Investual Relations).

8. There is an approach and an attitude which can lead you to making your own breaks—your own success.

9. There is no need to gamble to achieve investment success.

10. You can get to know your investment self (through the Investor Questionnaire). This simplifies the job of learning which traits to develop and which to avoid.

11. You should know just why you are involved in the stock market. If it is for gratifications which go beyond dollars and cents, you should understand this.

12. There is a way to see both the good and the bad in their proper perspective. And there is lots of money to be made from a programmed contrary opinion.

13. Understanding business in general is crucial —but not really complicated. In addition, there is a way by which we can assess the basic industries available for investment on a fairly objective basis—through the Industry Strength Guide.

14. We know what others do not comprehend—about business in general as well as about ourselves —and frankly we can benefit from this.

15. Imagination is so important—and it can be

developed into part of one's investing arsenal.

16. There are stocks to be bought and lived with, and there are those which are bought to be sold. Disciplines exist which help to distinguish between these categories and to aid in the timing of purchases and sales.

17. We understand the difference between patience and stubbornness, indecision, laziness, and inertia—and we comprehend the wisdom of staying around for the big profits.

18. There is a way to structure portfolios so as to achieve growth without undue exposure (and without overdiversification).

19. It is not difficult to know what to do with money once you get it.

Yes, there is an overall method of thinking which should now be a part of you and which should place you in a superior competitive position with respect to other investors. Merely understanding your own investment personality and temperament along with the right kind of overall philosophy should ensure an unusual success pattern. While it is true that you cannot control the stock market itself, *you can control yourself* and this ability will place you way ahead of your competition.

So start now to put Psycho-Cybernetics to work in the stock market. Understand the positive inputs presented to you and practice them until they become a part of your psyche, a part of your intuitive powers.

In my previous two books, I concluded with a typical "Good Luck" to my readers—but no longer! Whereas luck will play some part in the future (see chapter 12), my final advice to you is now different. You have the capabilities for real success. The answer lies upstairs in that mind of yours and in proper inputs.

You were what you were, but that is not what you are now!

Good inputs . . . good outputs.

ABOUT THE AUTHOR

Described by *Barron's* as "an expert, a proven investment practitioner and a professional's professional," Claude Rosenberg, Jr., has had a uniquely successful career as a financial analyst and money manager. He pioneered the concept of in-depth regional research (for J. Barth & Co. of San Francisco) and built one of the best-respected research organizations in the country. For years he wrote a bi-weekly market comment which was highly regarded by both individual and institutional investors for its frankness and honesty, as well as for its record of analyzing the stock market in general and for a consistent job of individual stock selection. In addition, he authored two books previous to *Psycho-Cybernetics and the Stock Market*, both of which were extremely well received and which established his common-sense approach to investing. He has lectured extensively on the field of investments and has been widely quoted in numerous national publications.

After fifteen years with J. Barth & Co., Mr. Rosenberg formed, in 1970, his own investment advisory operation in San Francisco (Rosenberg Capital Management). A graduate of Stanford University, where he holds both B.A. (Economics) and M.B.A. degrees, he is President of the Stanford Business School Alumni Association and has been active in various organizations in the San Francisco Bay Area.